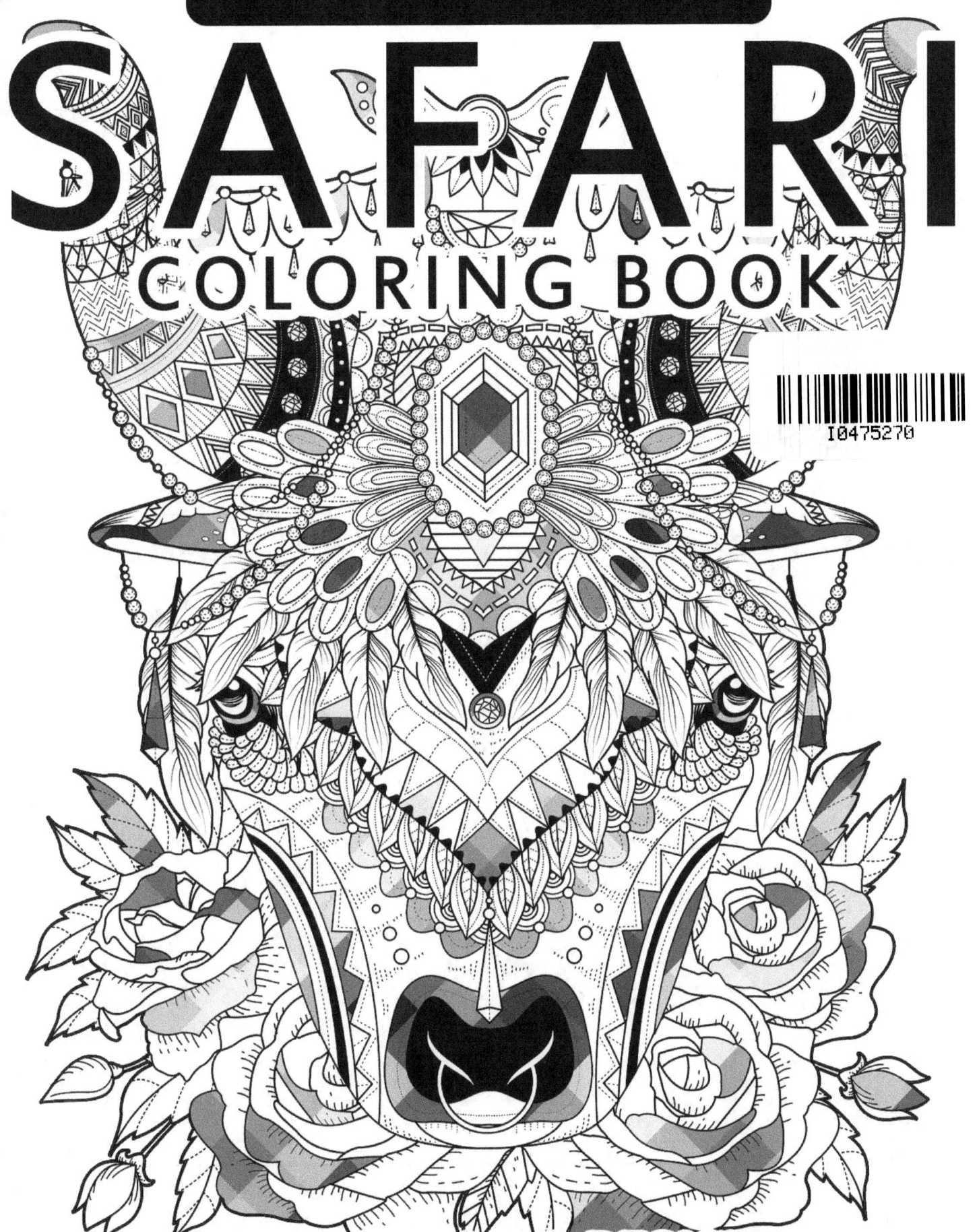

STRESS RELIEVING
SAFARI
COLORING BOOK

WILD ANIMALS DESIGNS

TEST YOUR COLOR

TEST YOUR COLOR

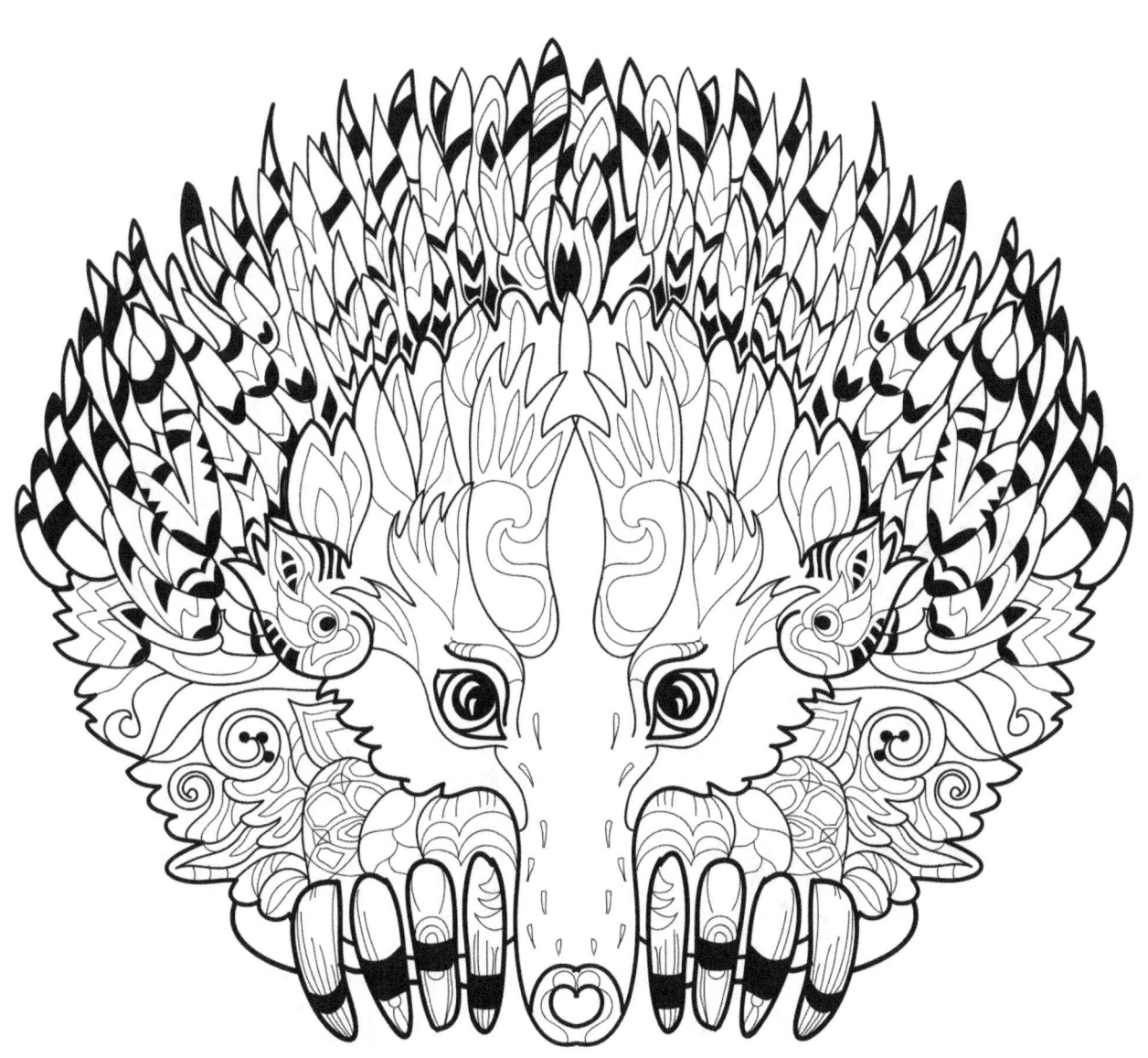

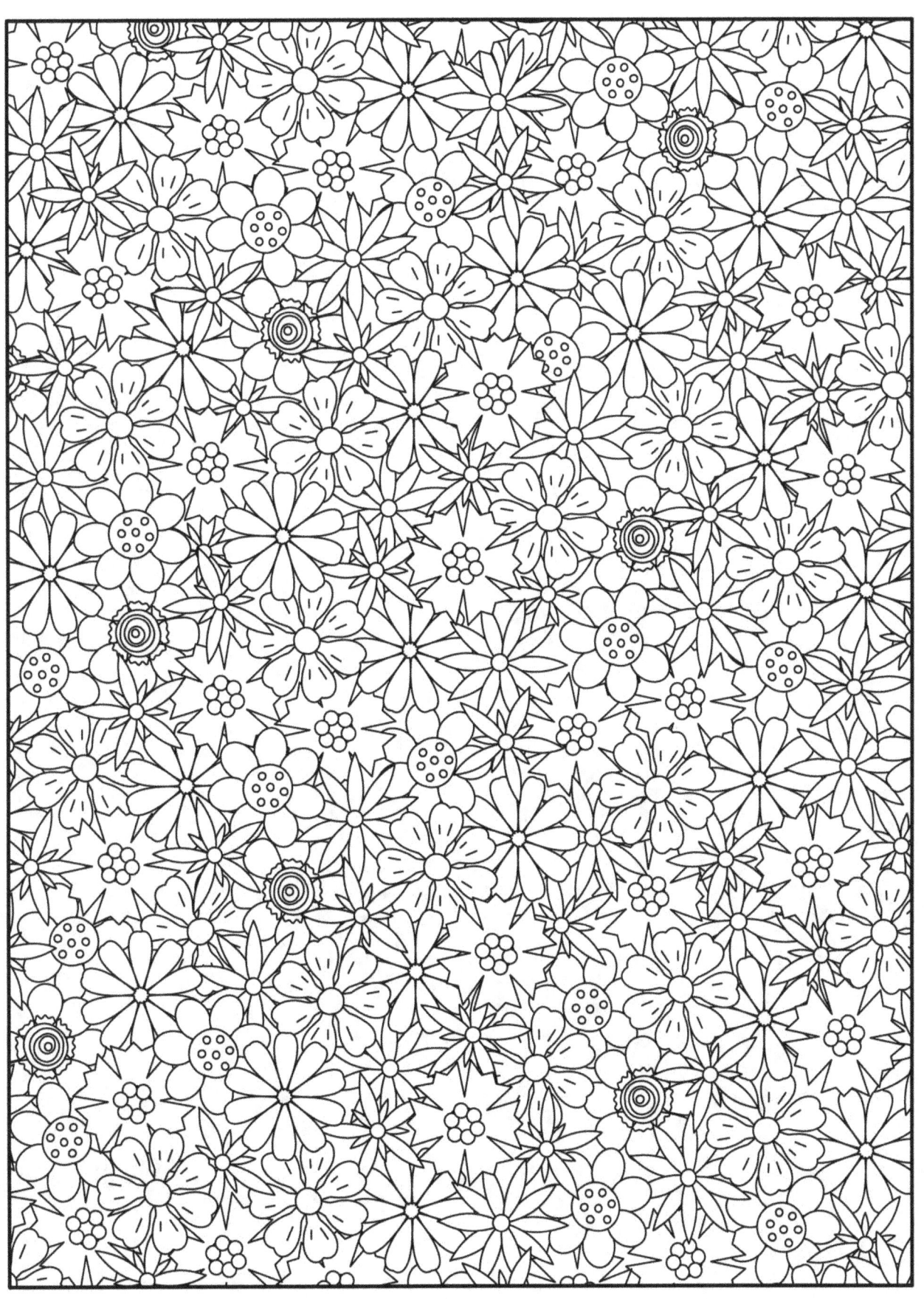

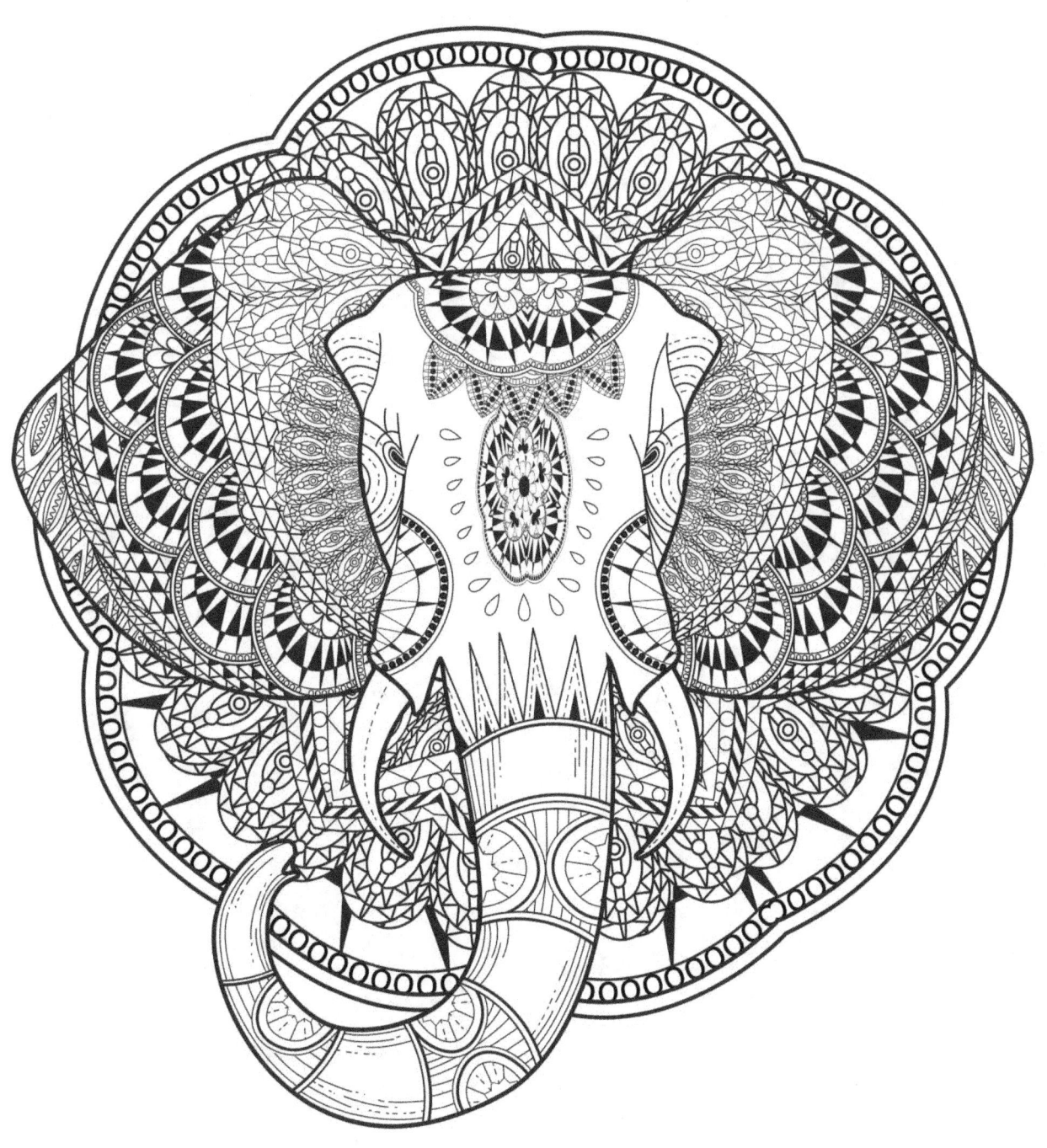

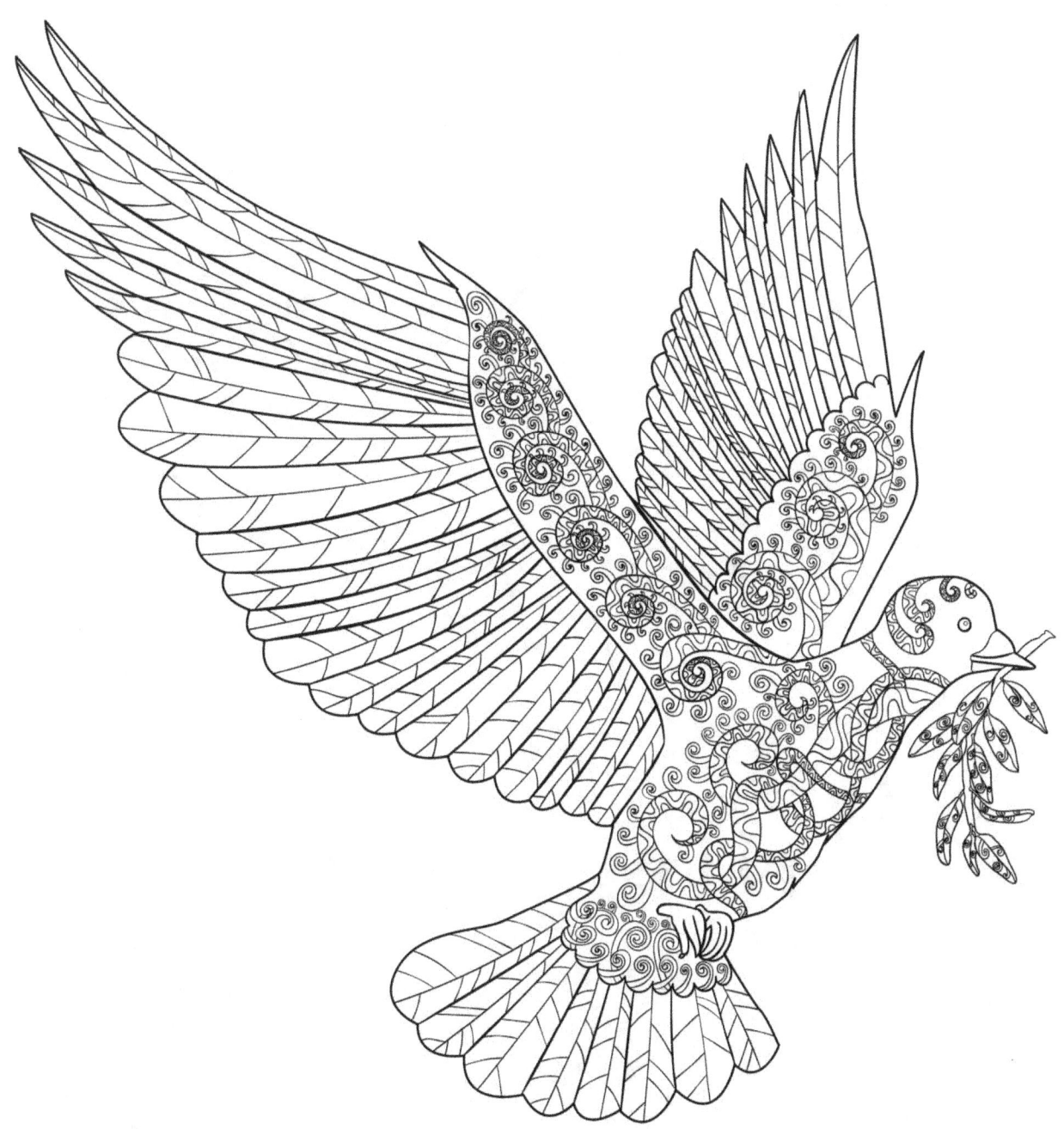

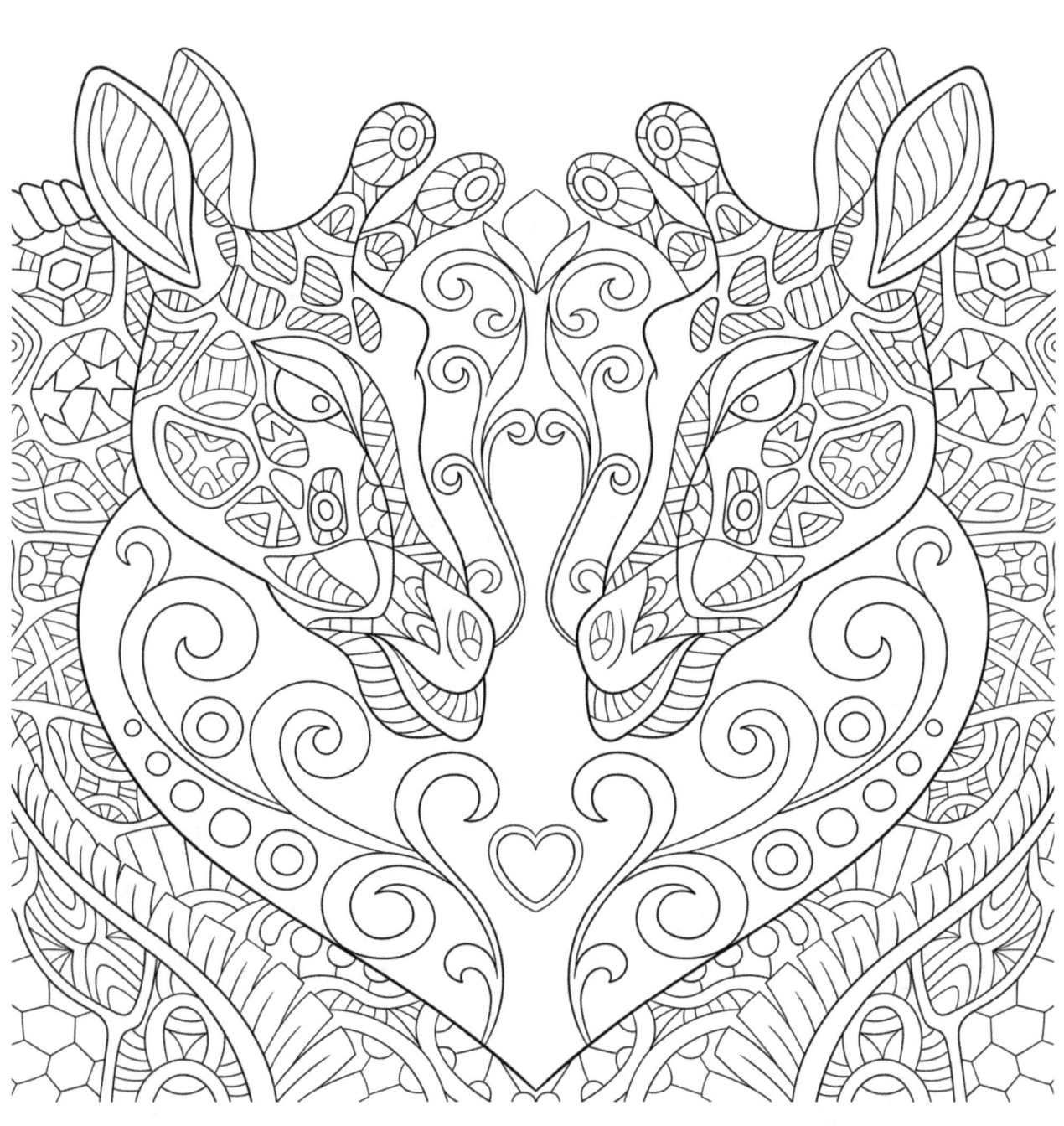

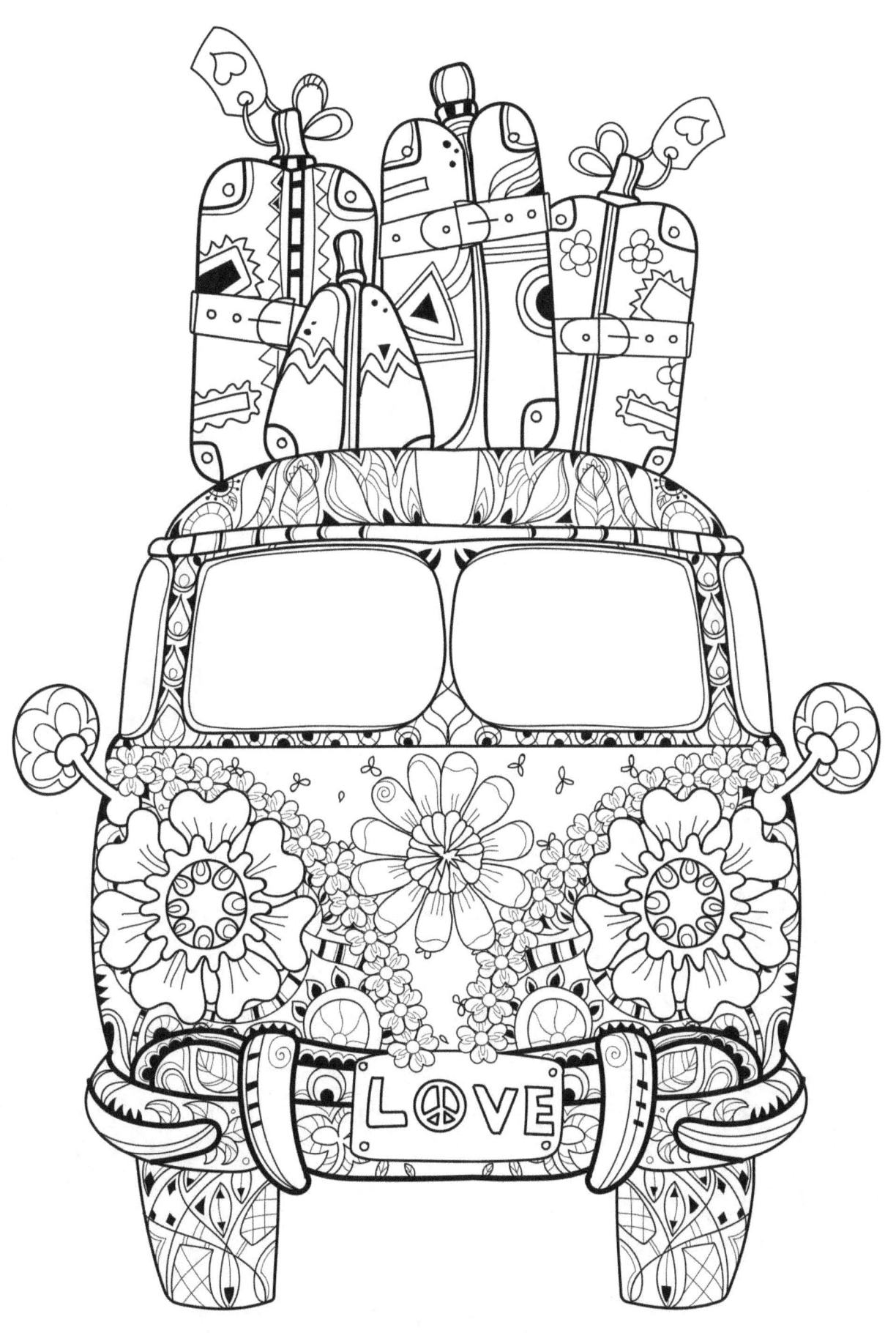

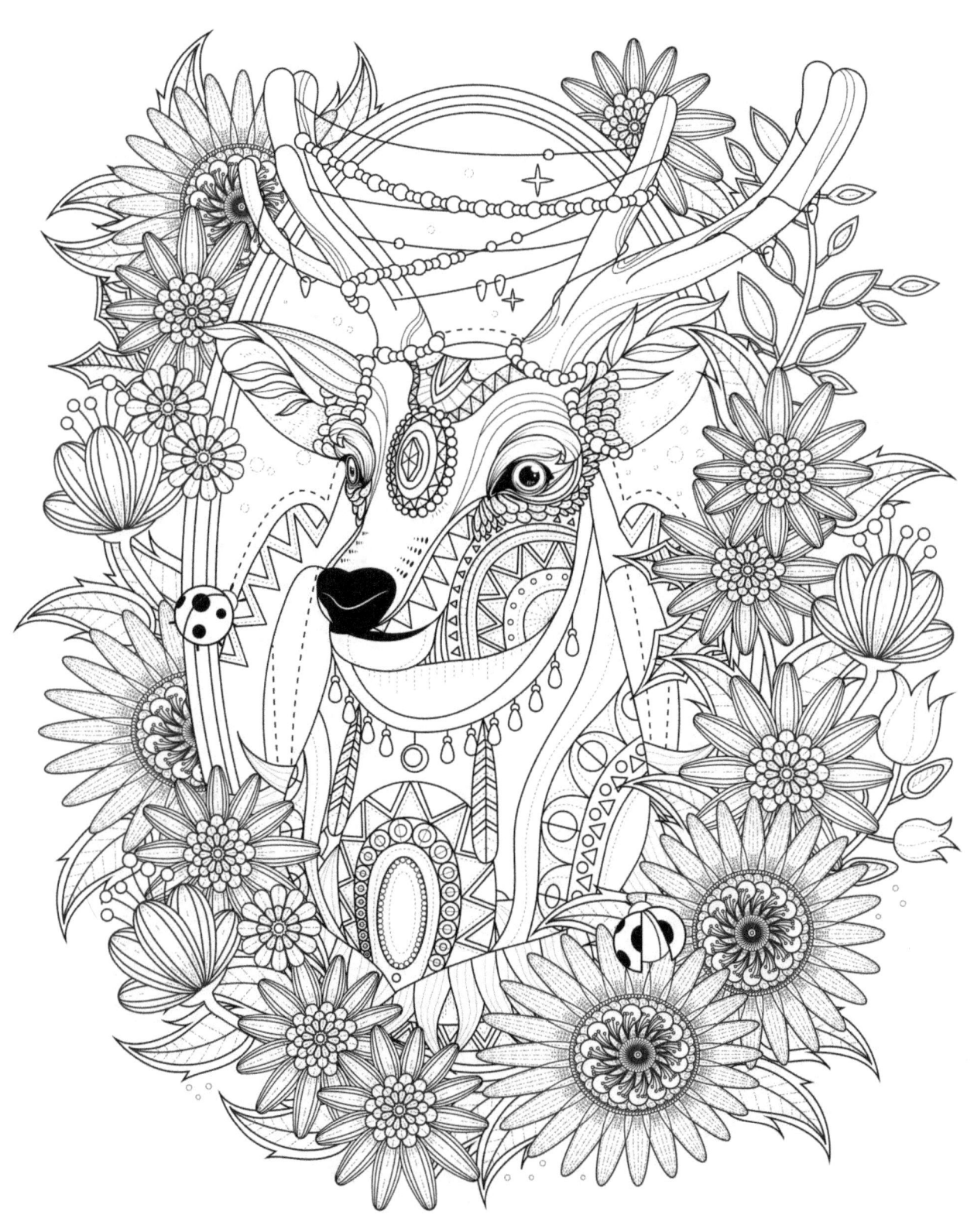

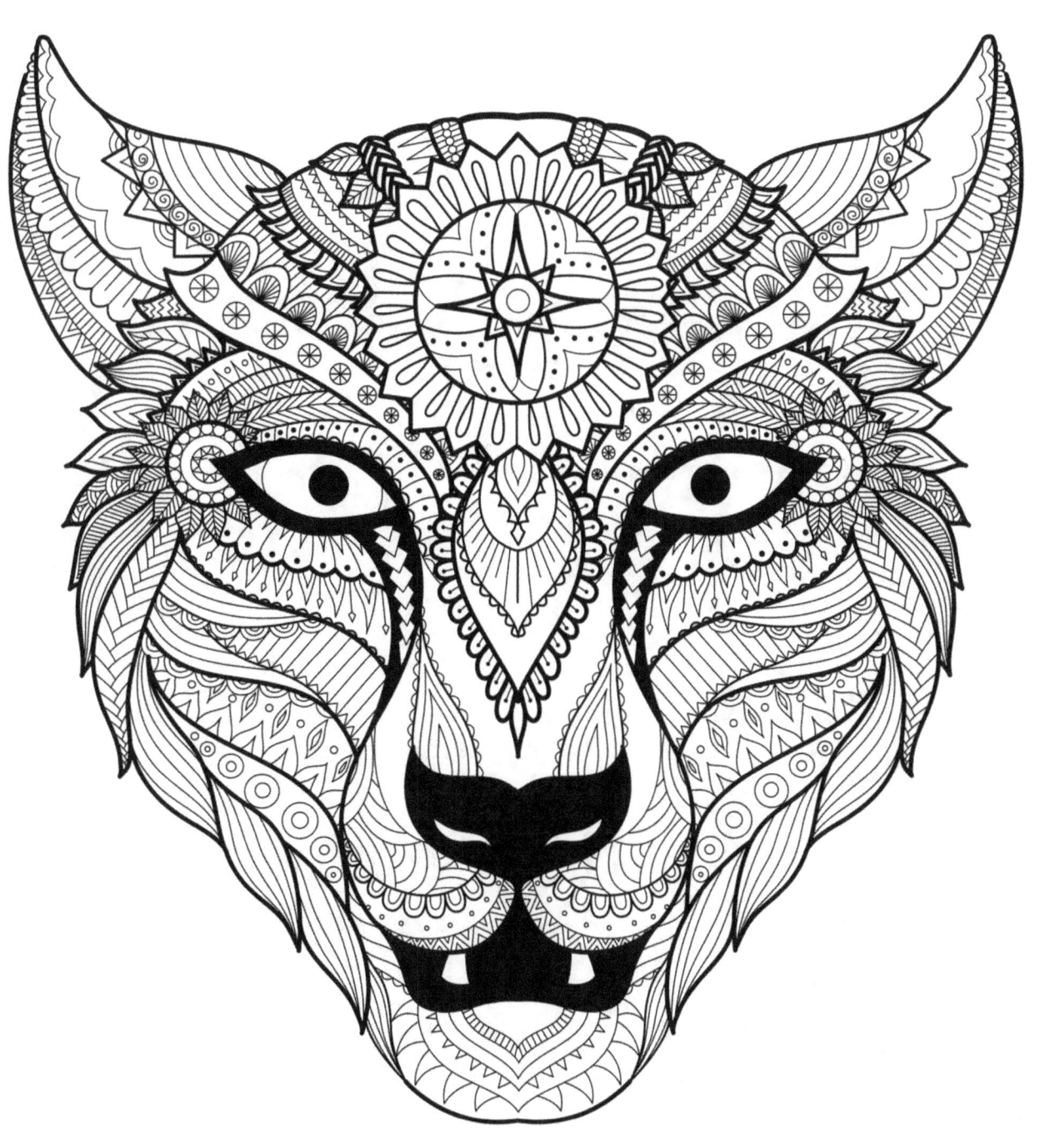

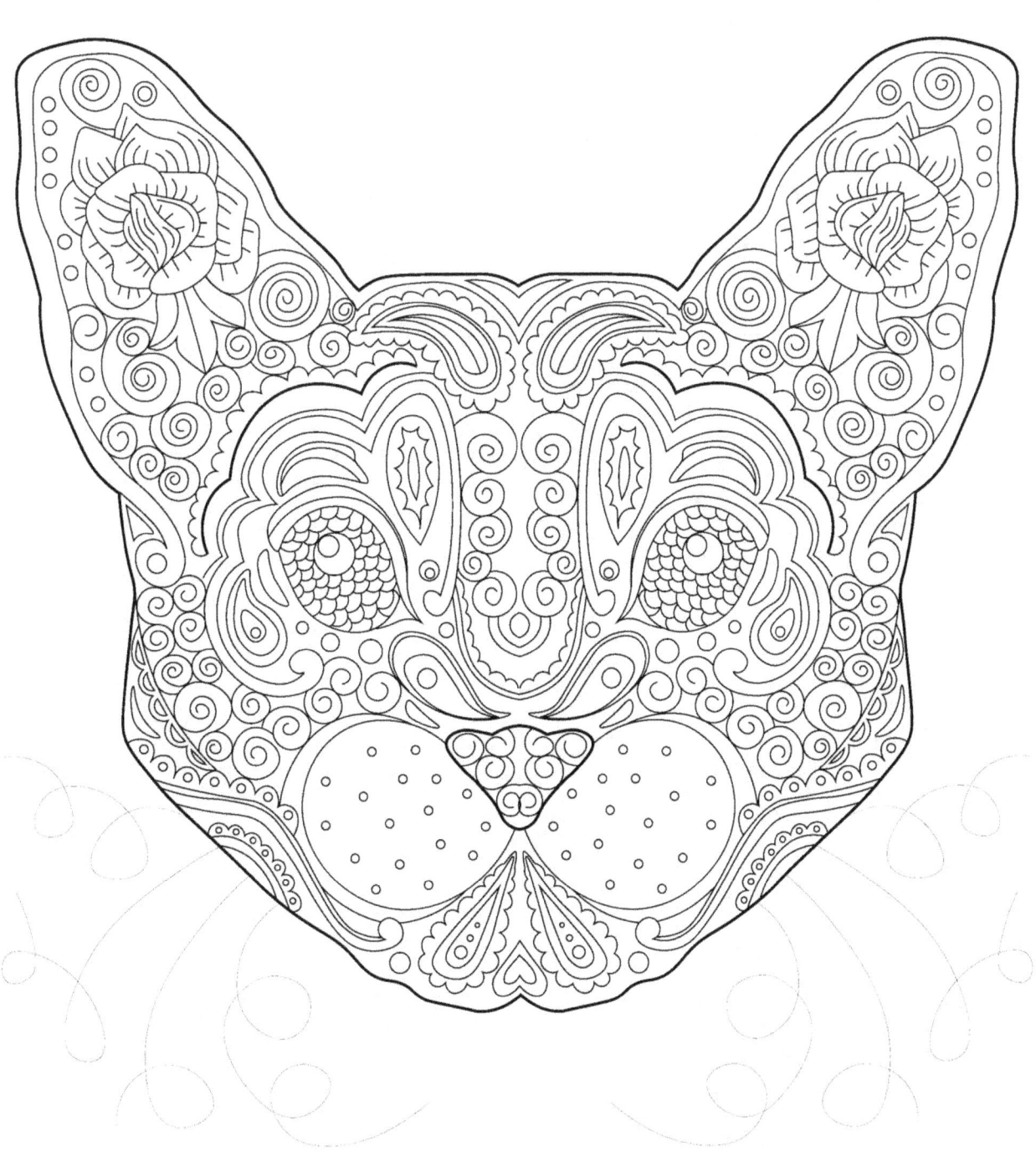

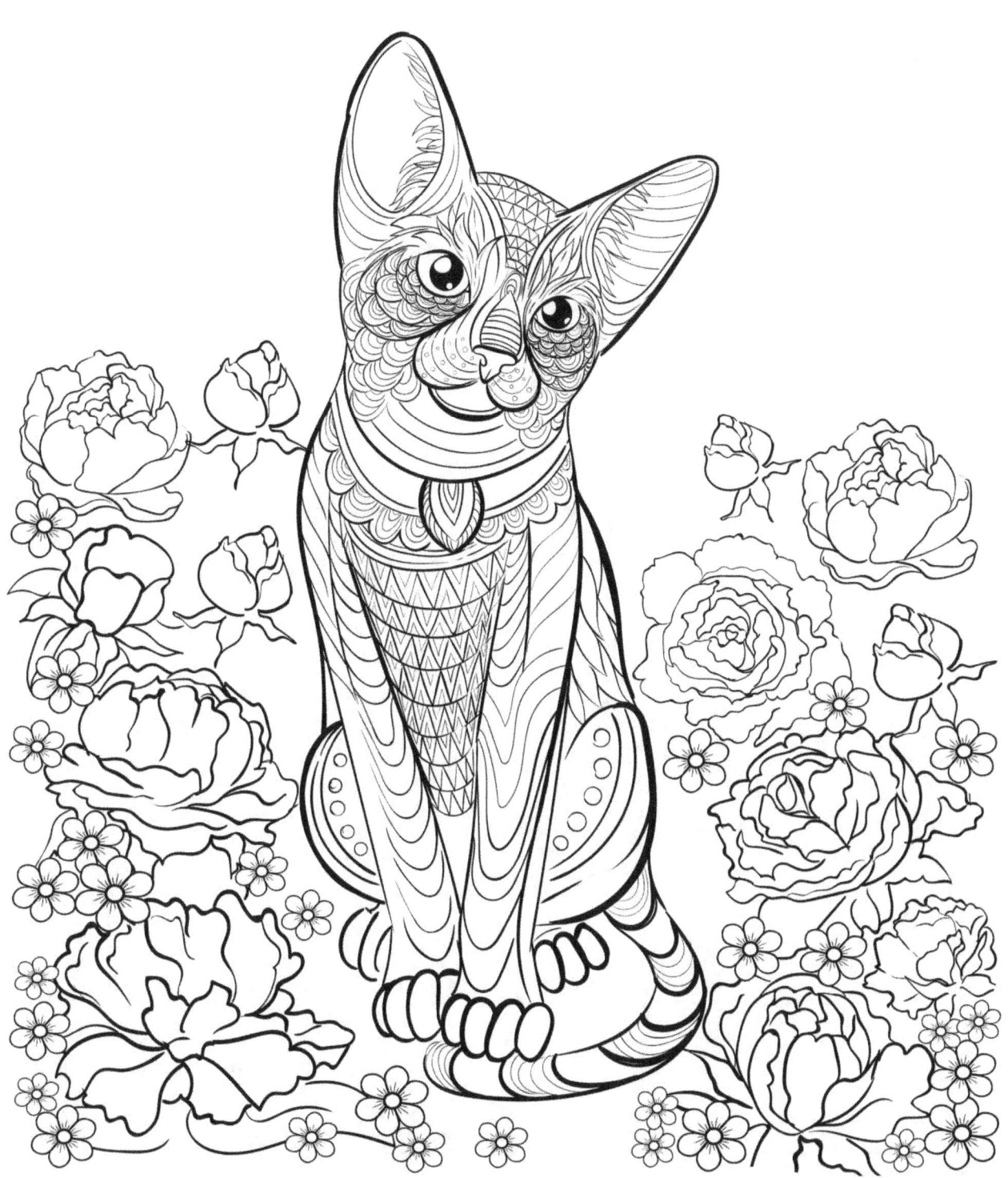

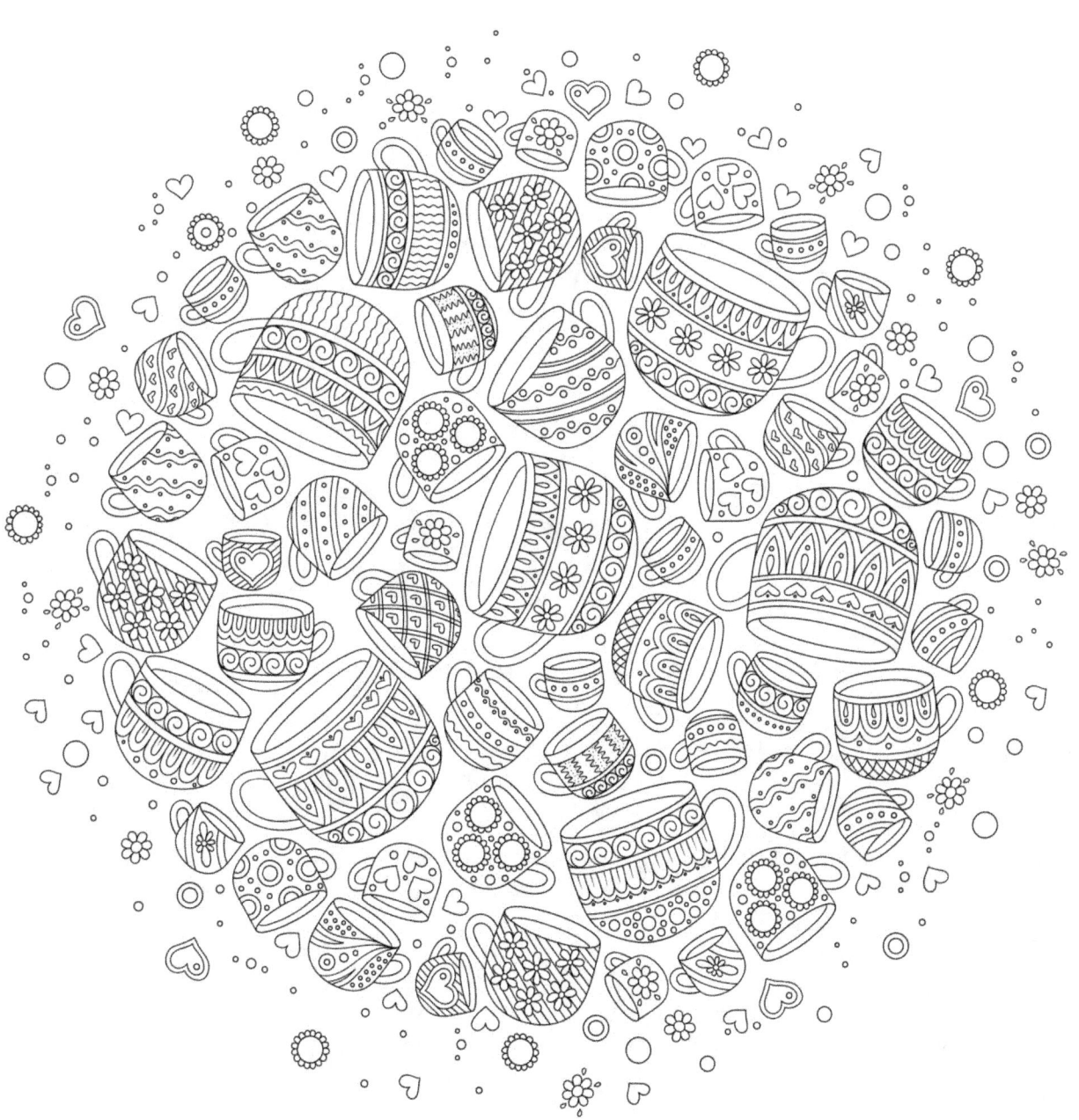

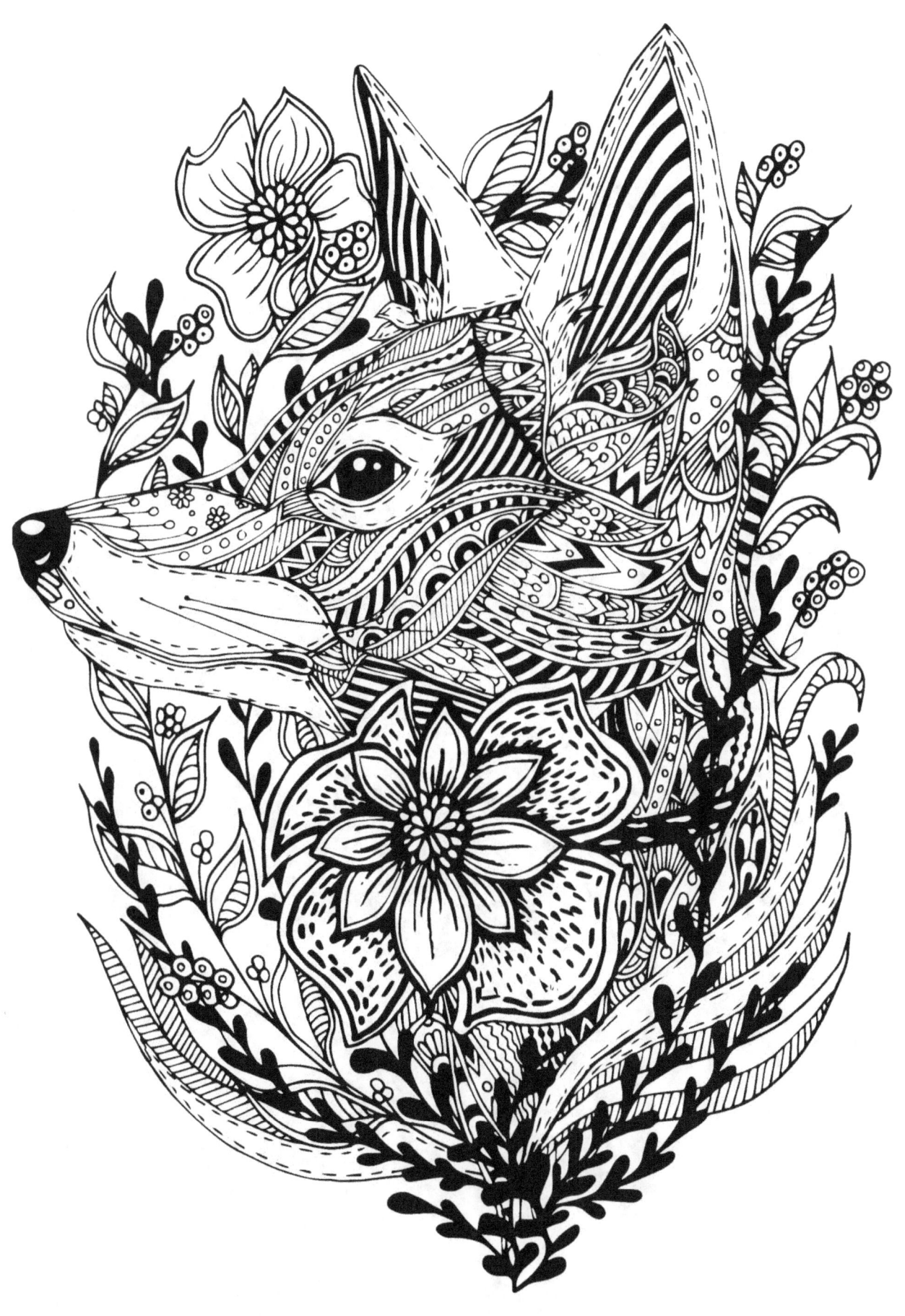

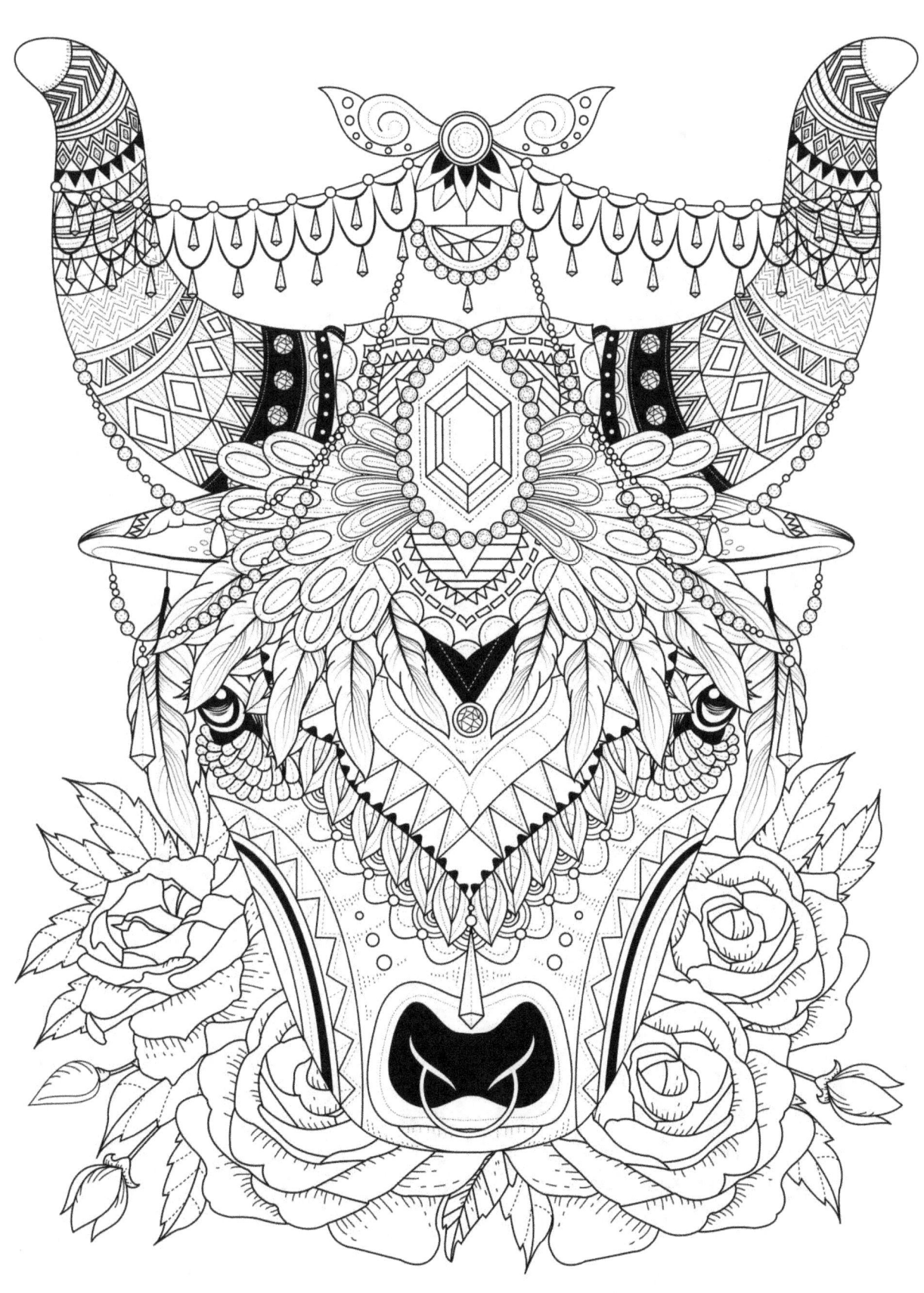

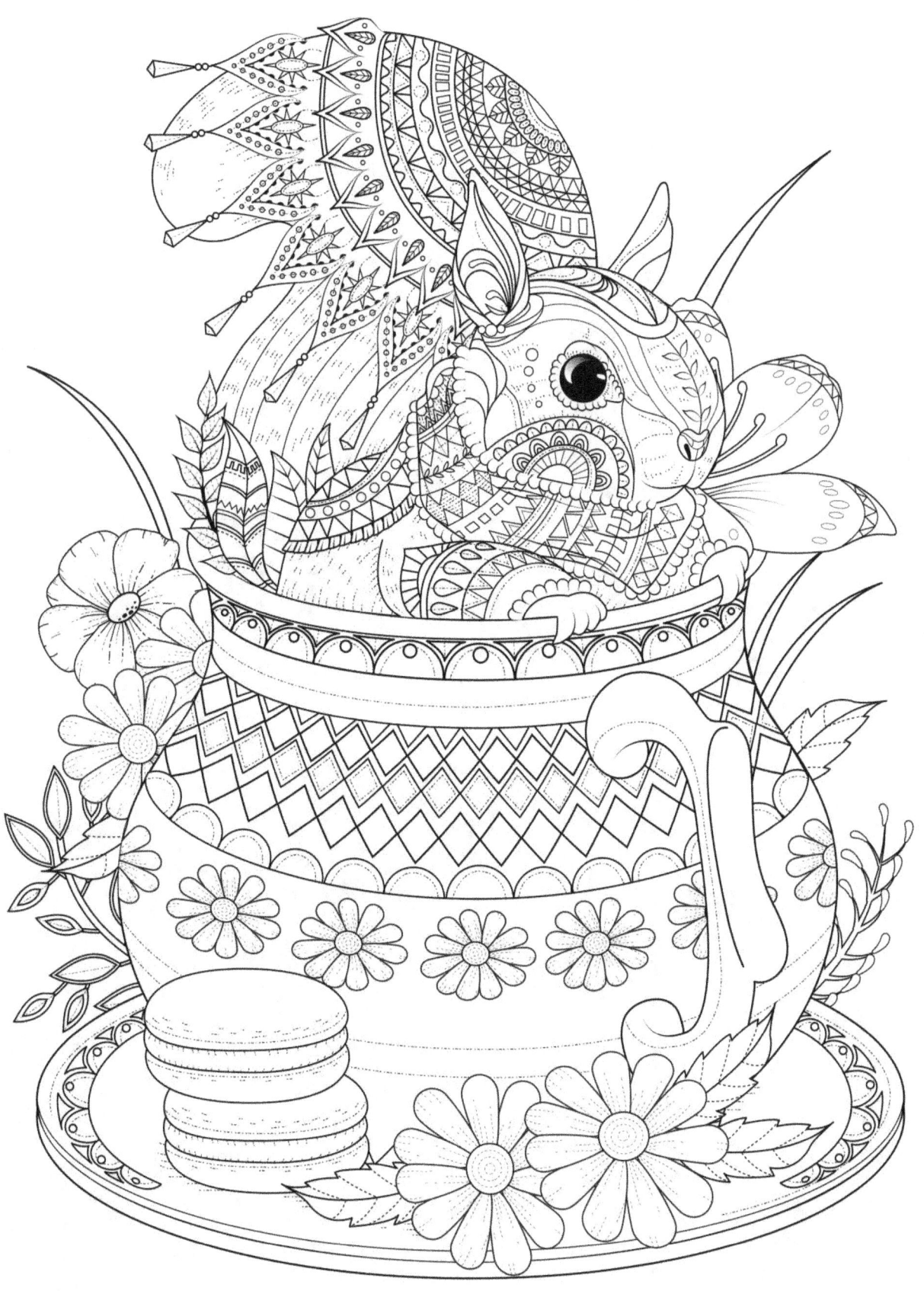

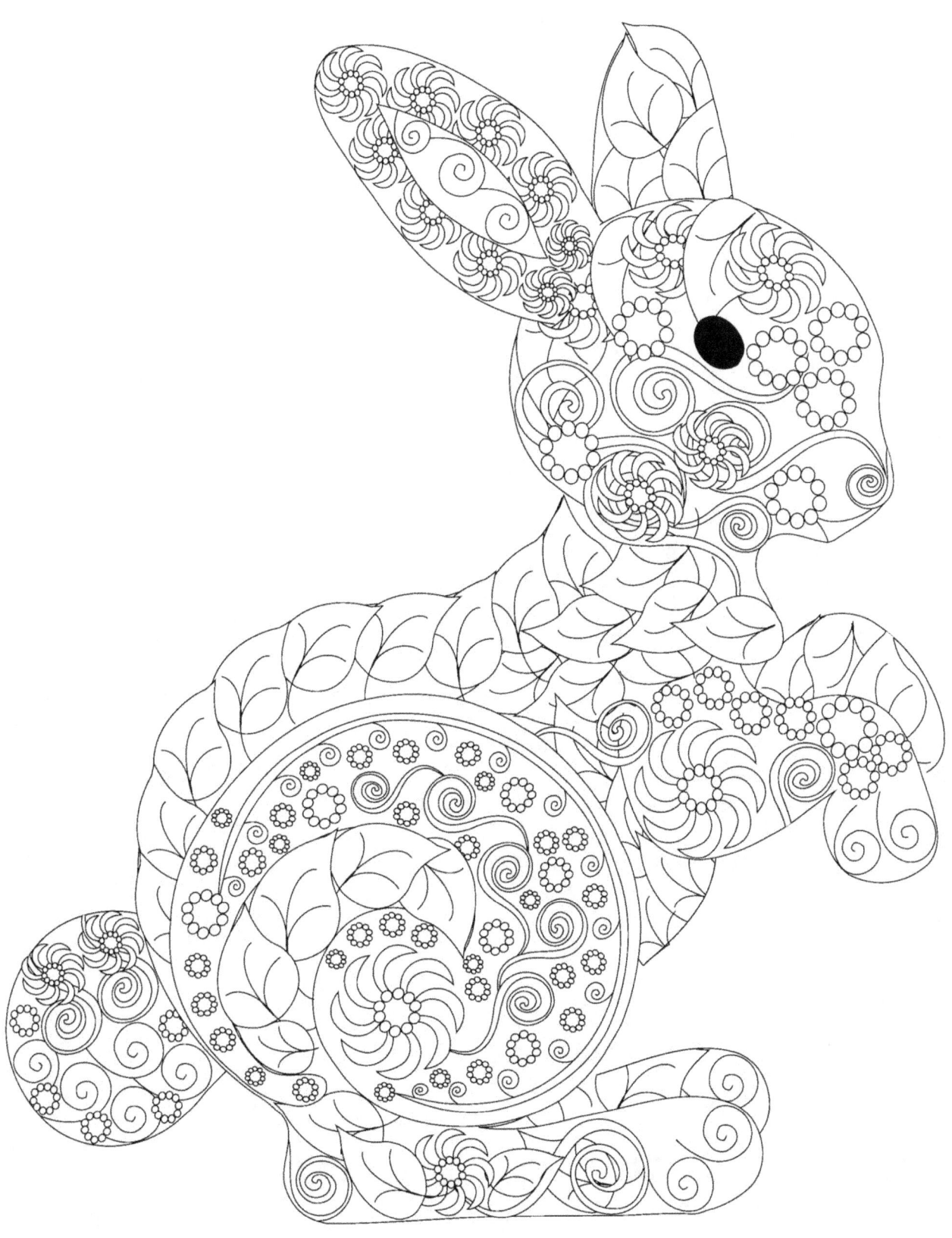

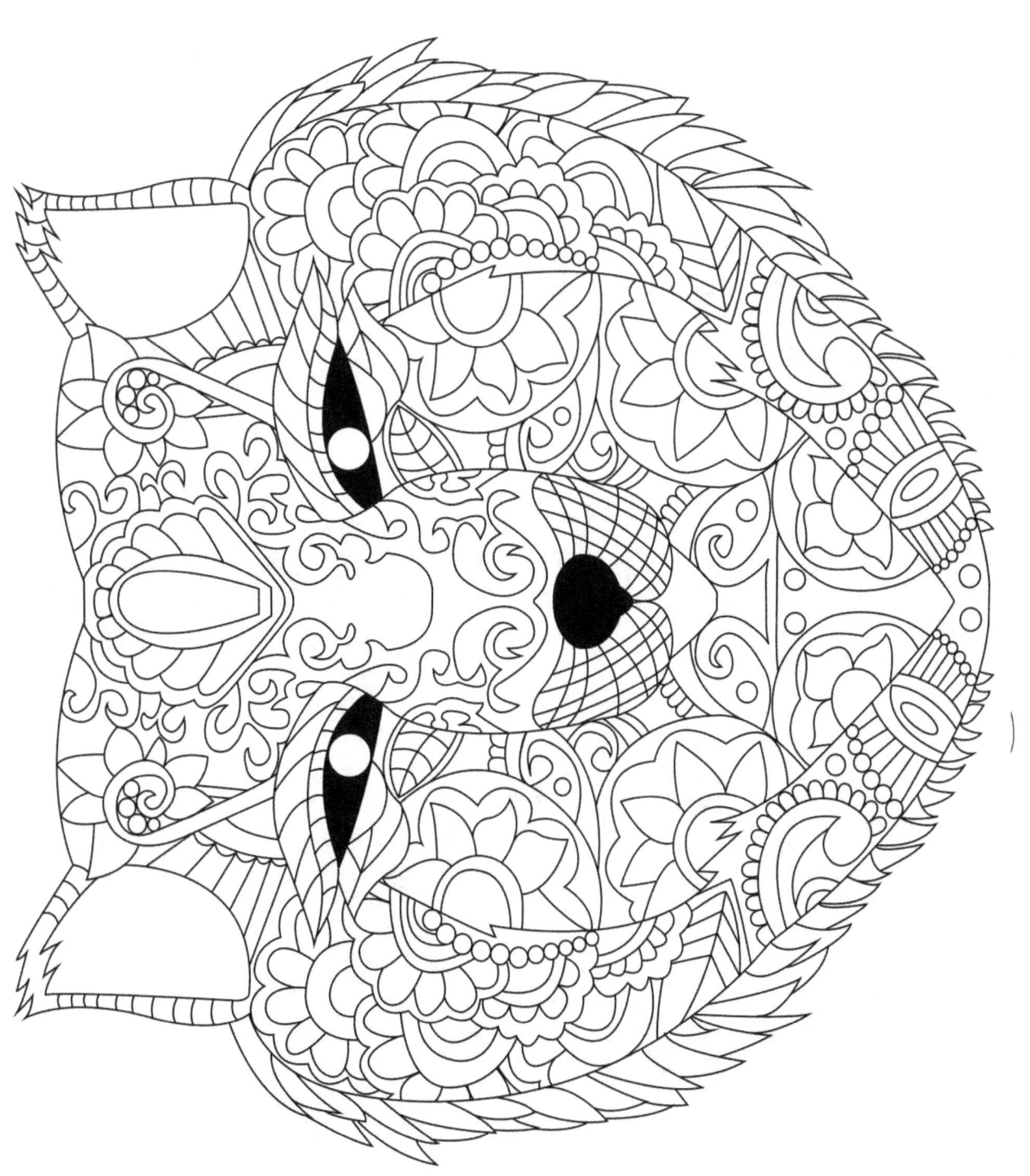

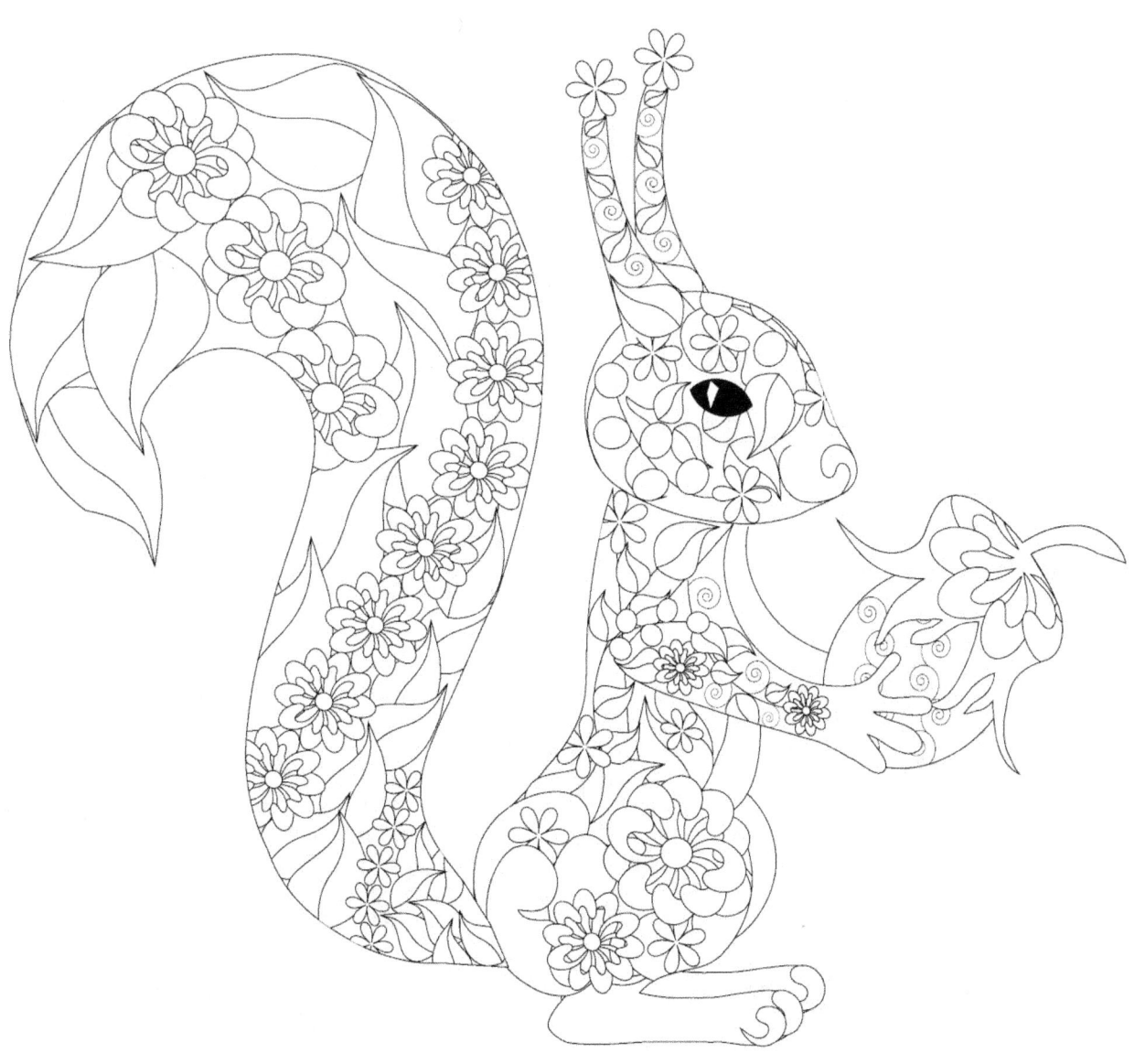

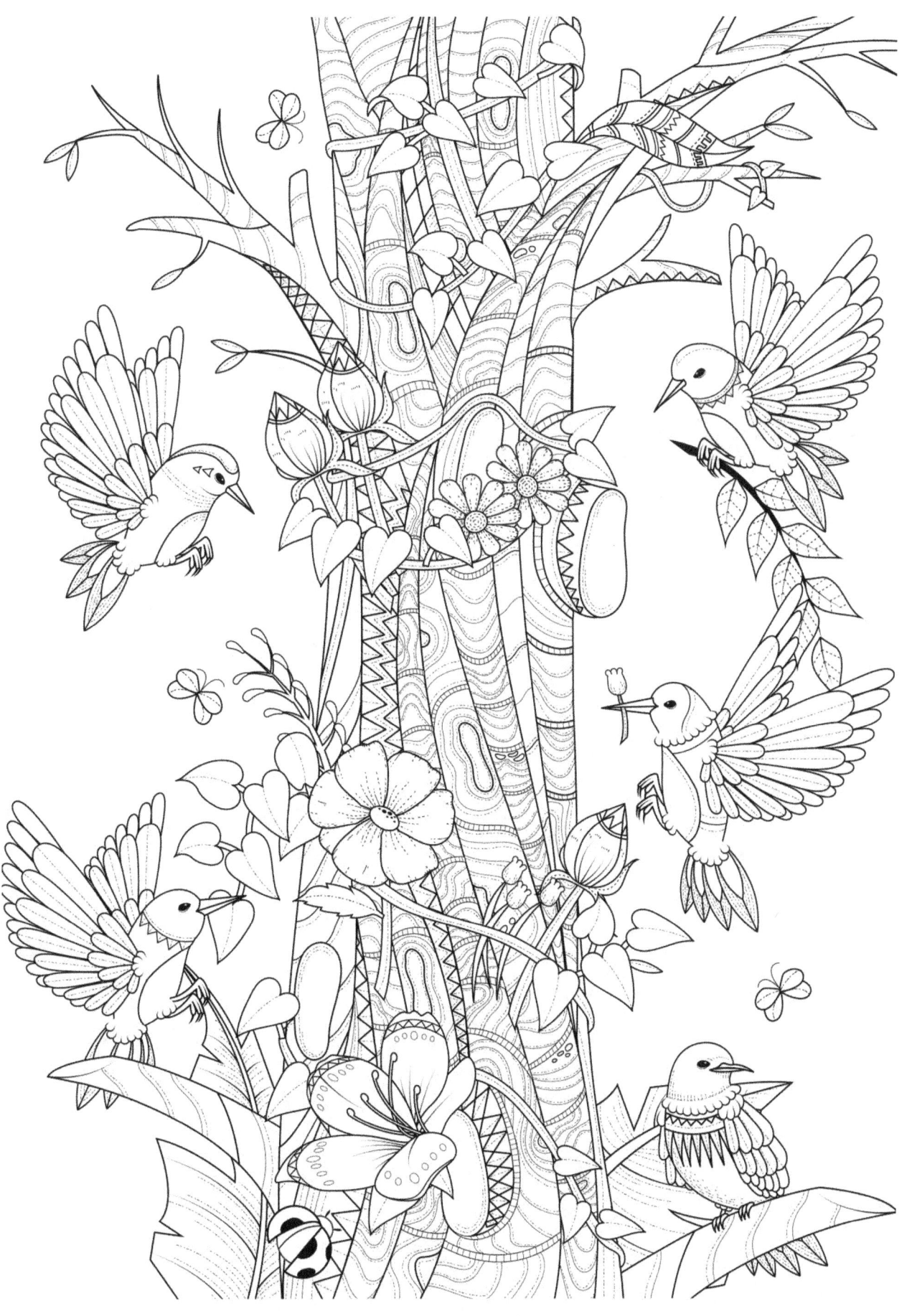

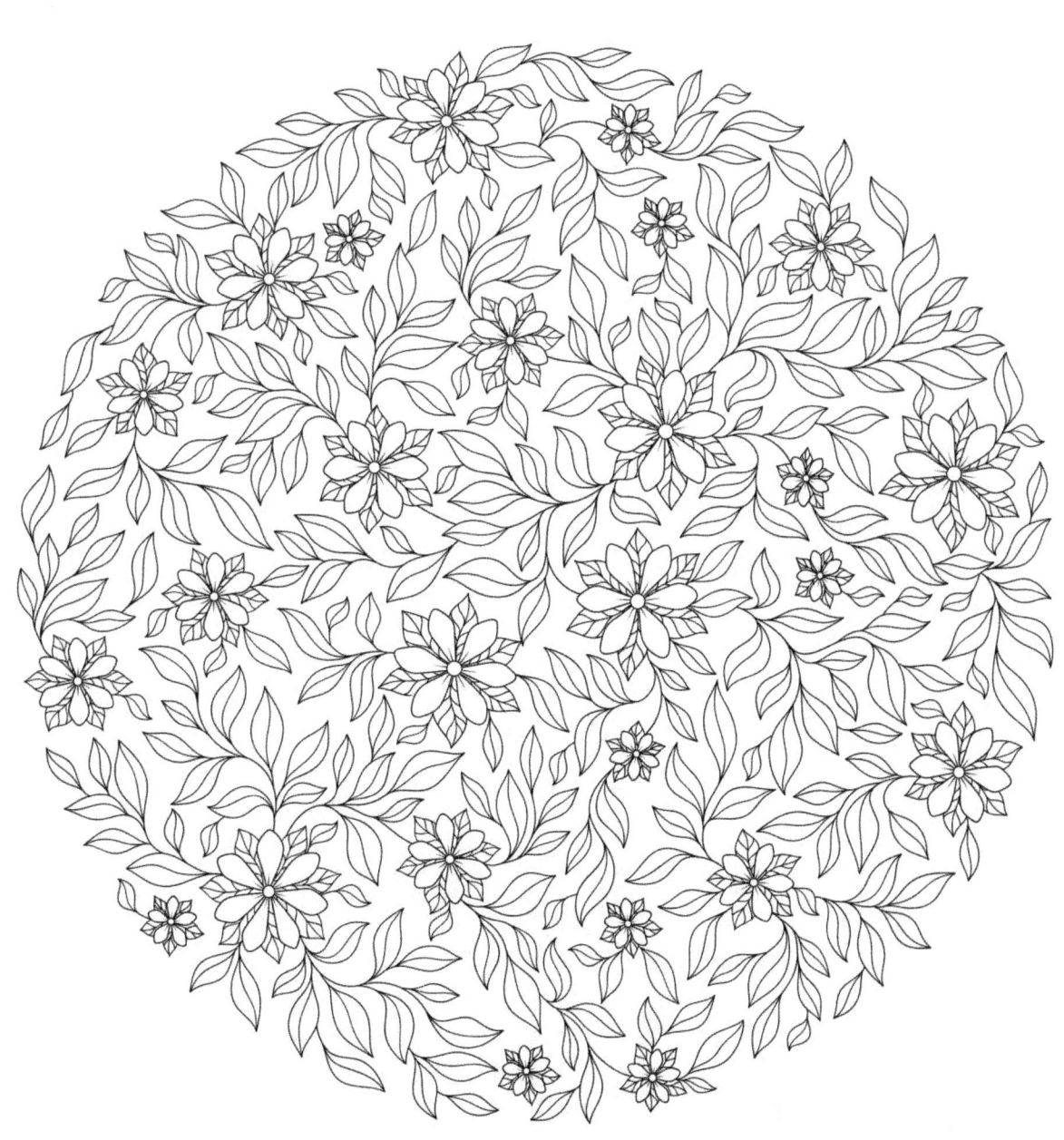

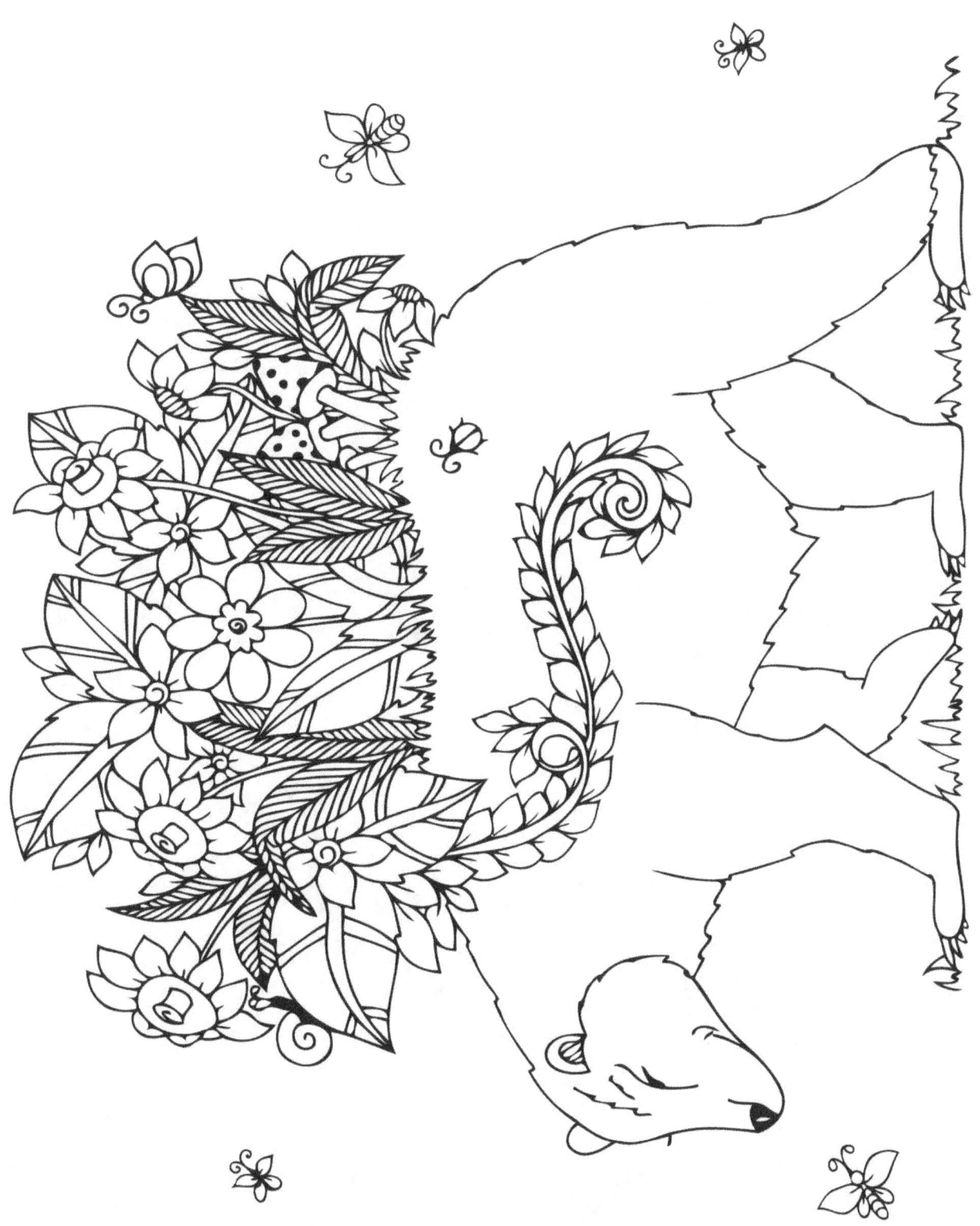

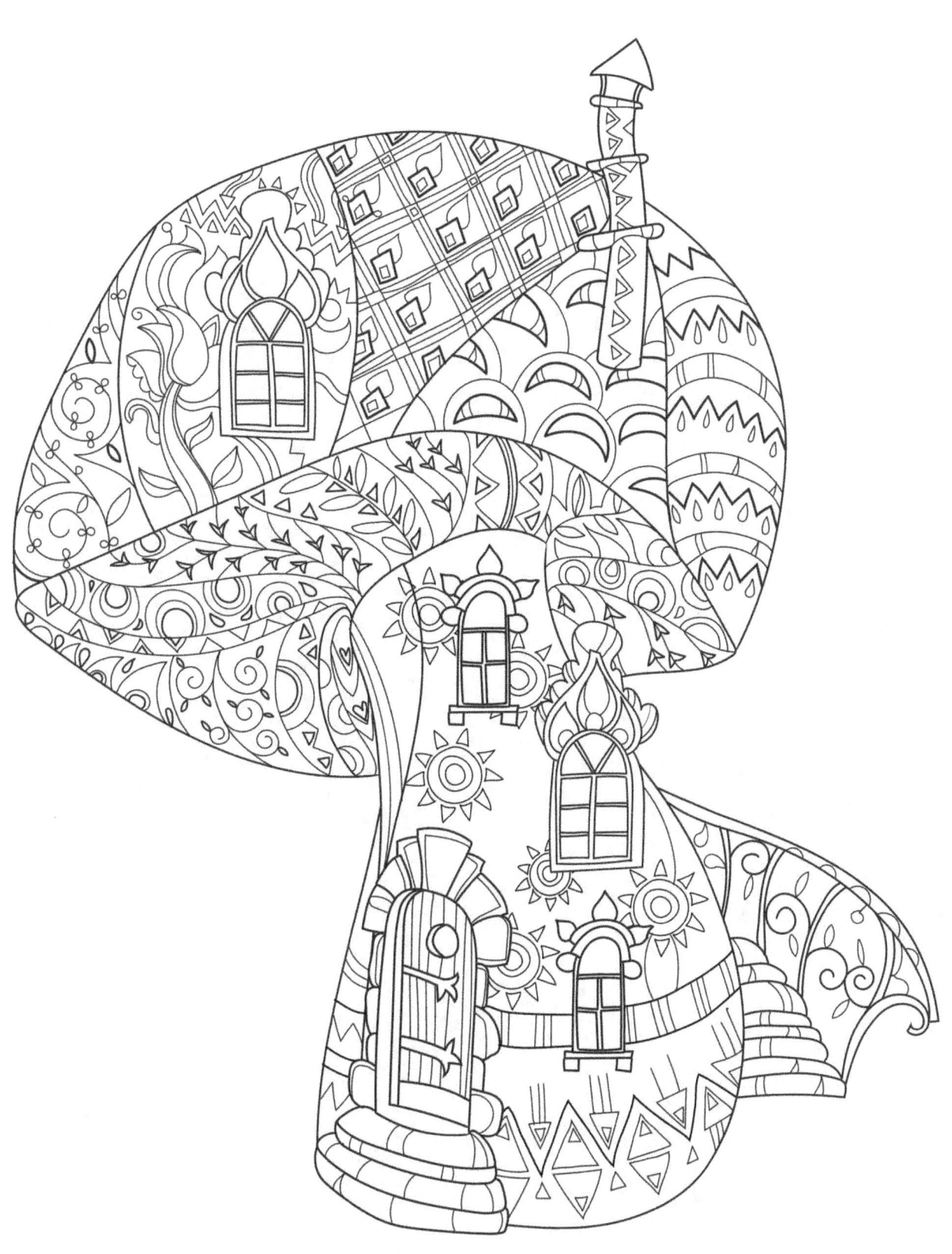

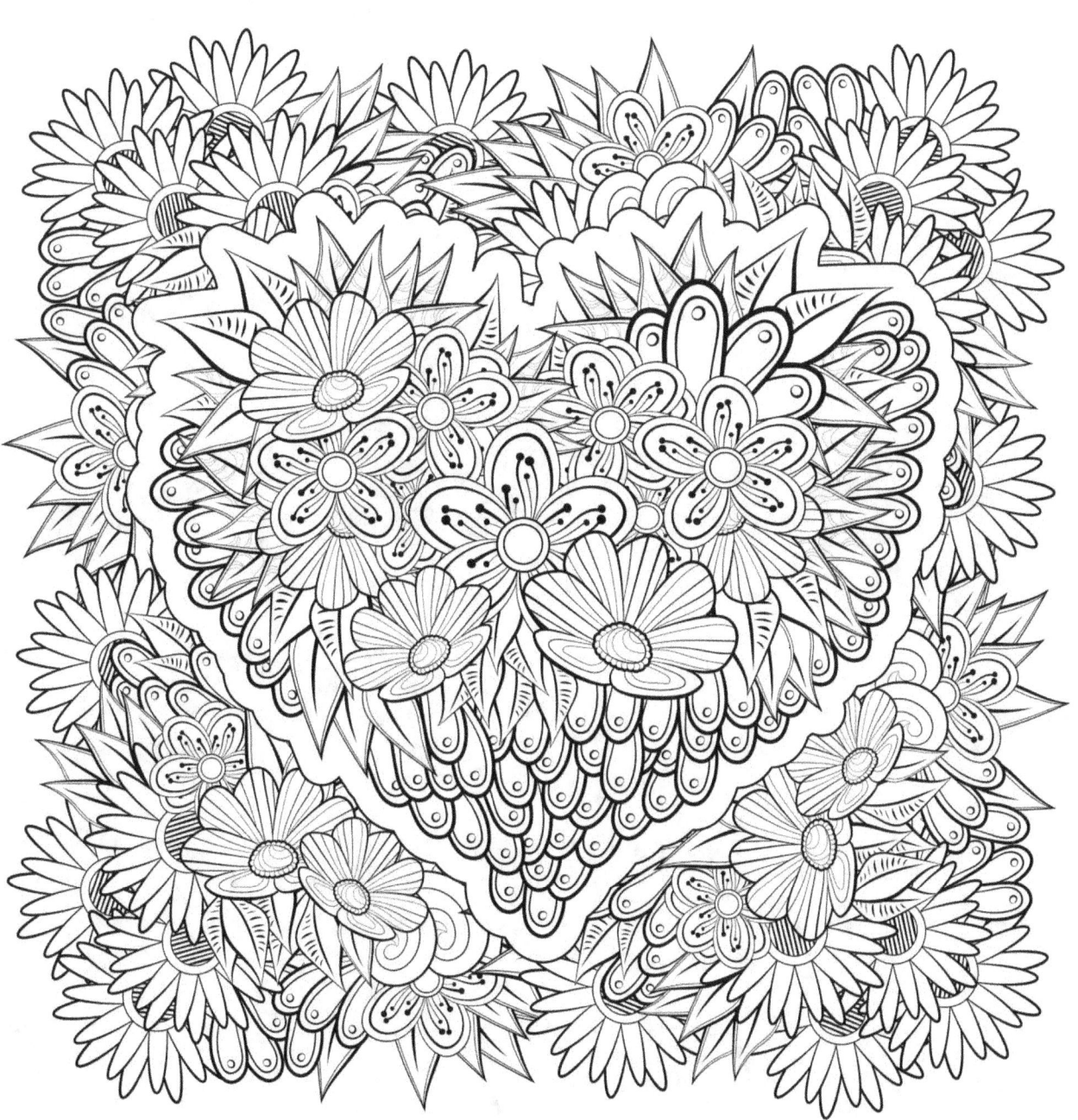

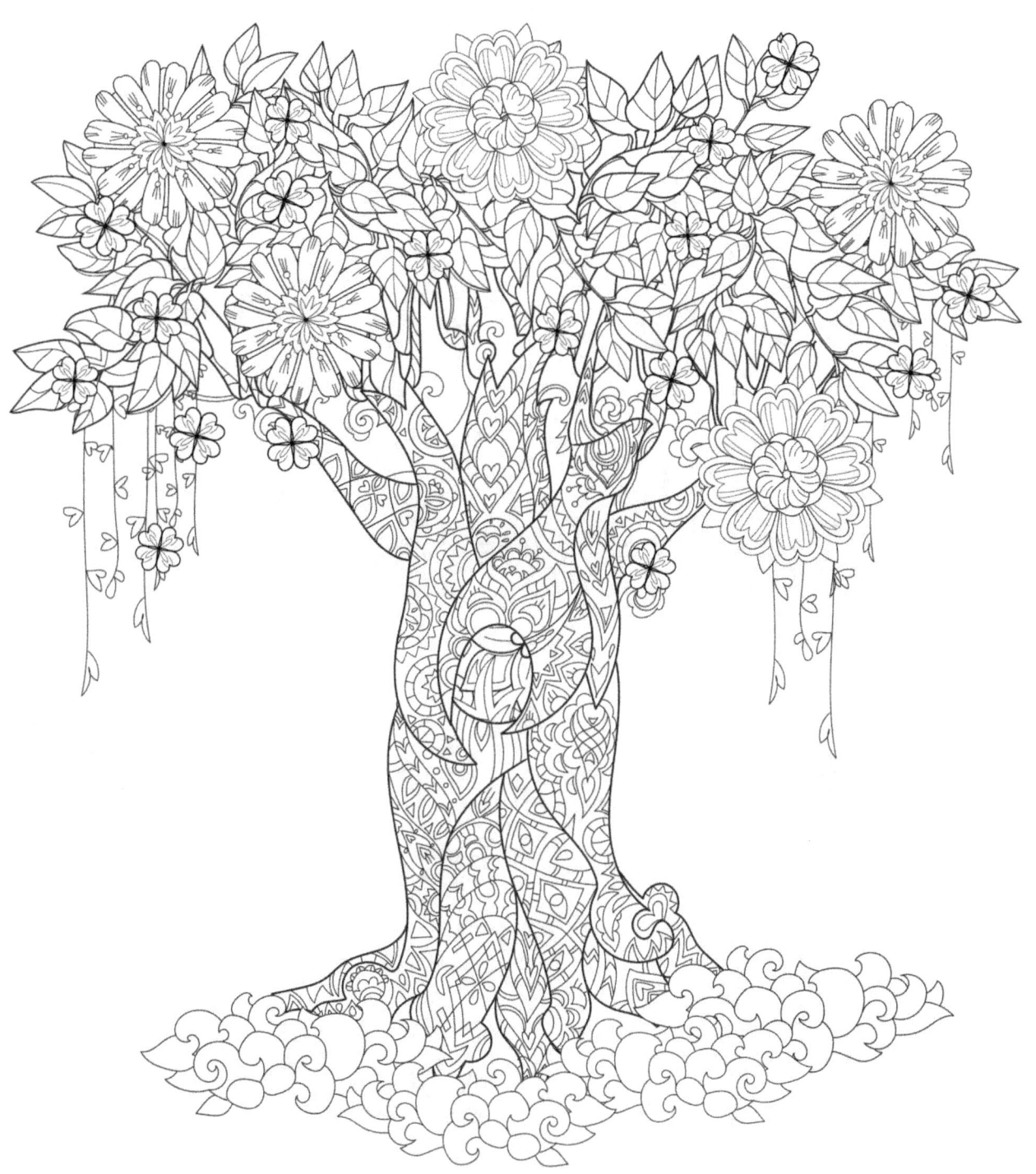

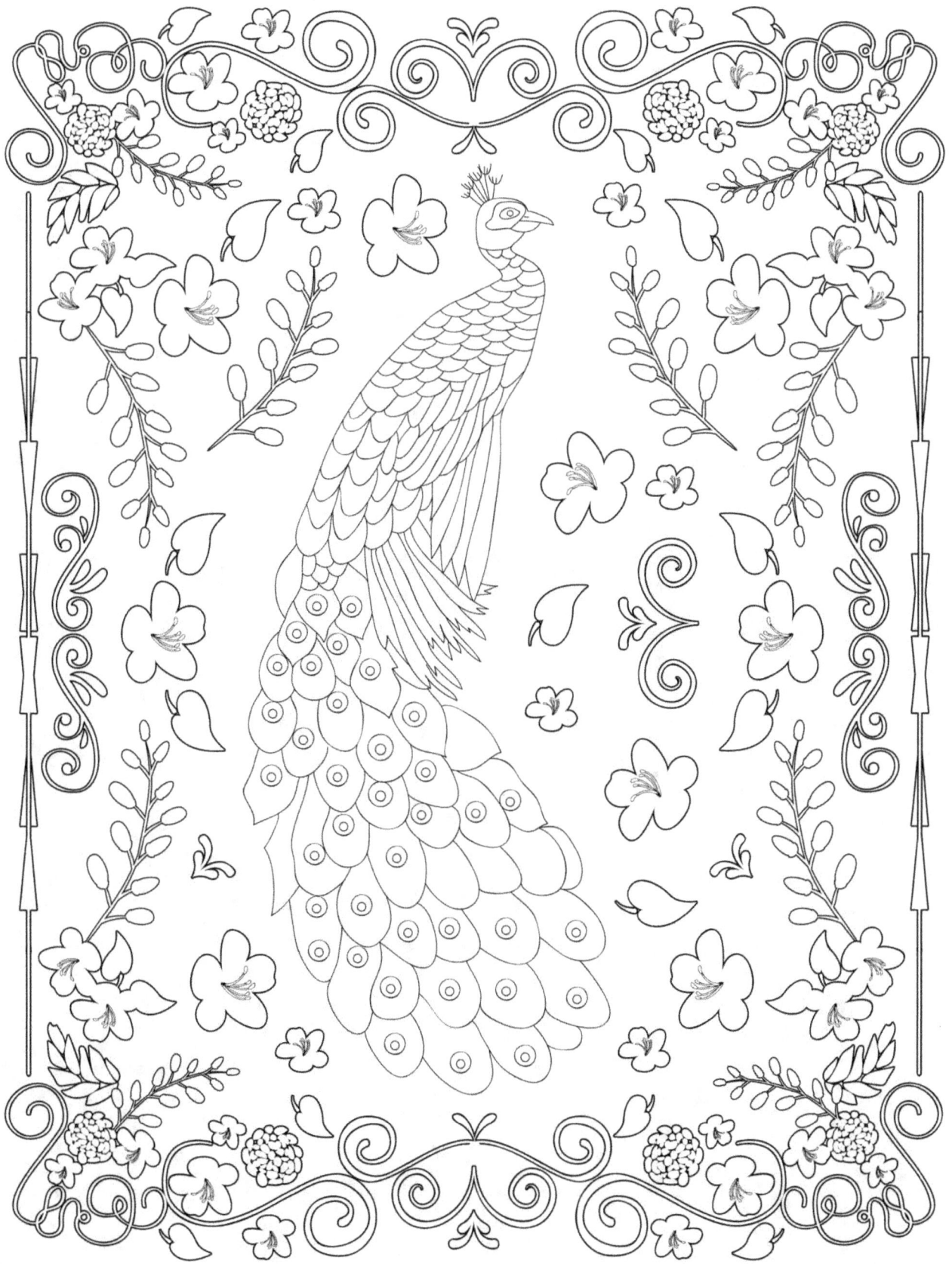

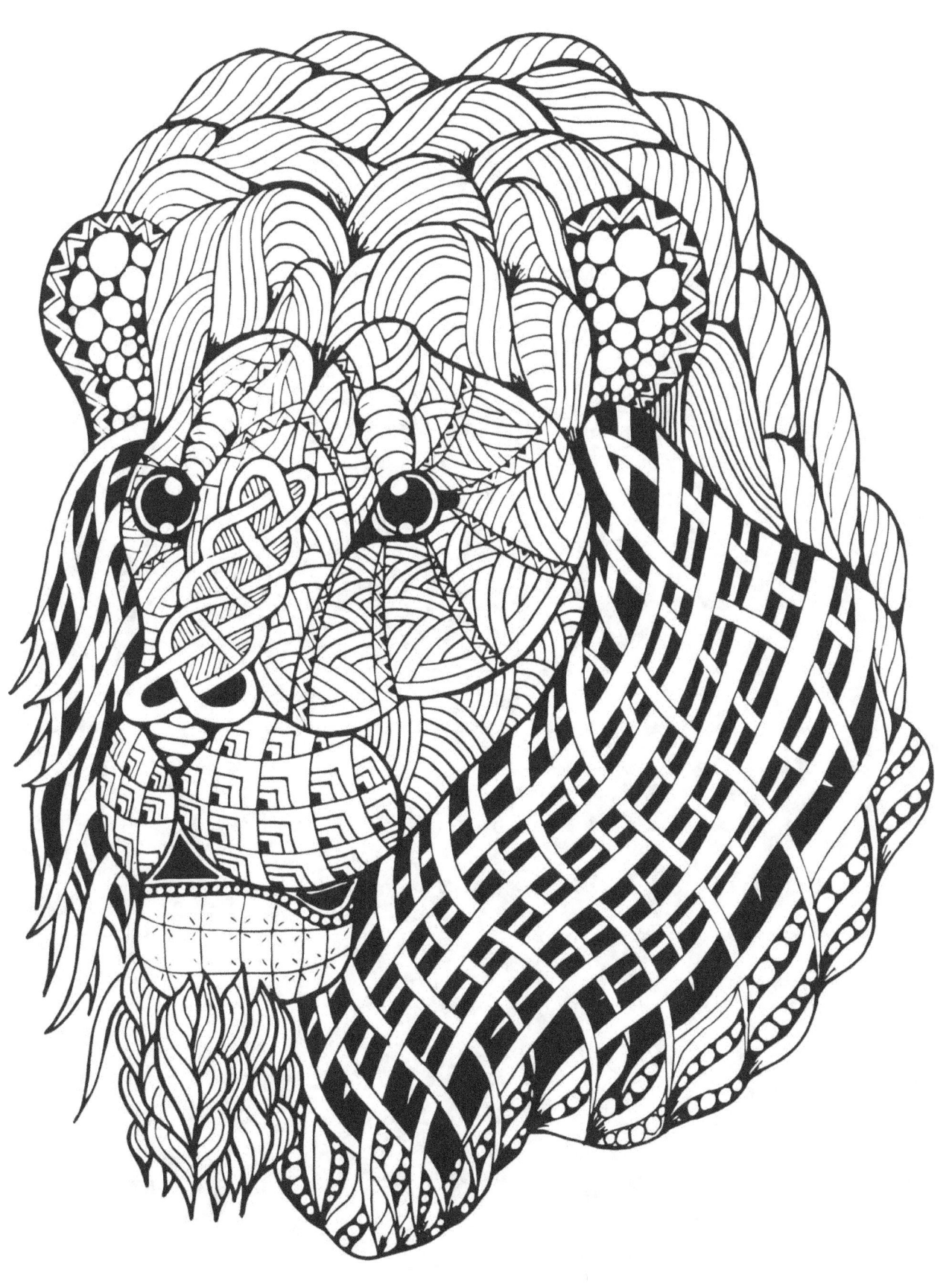

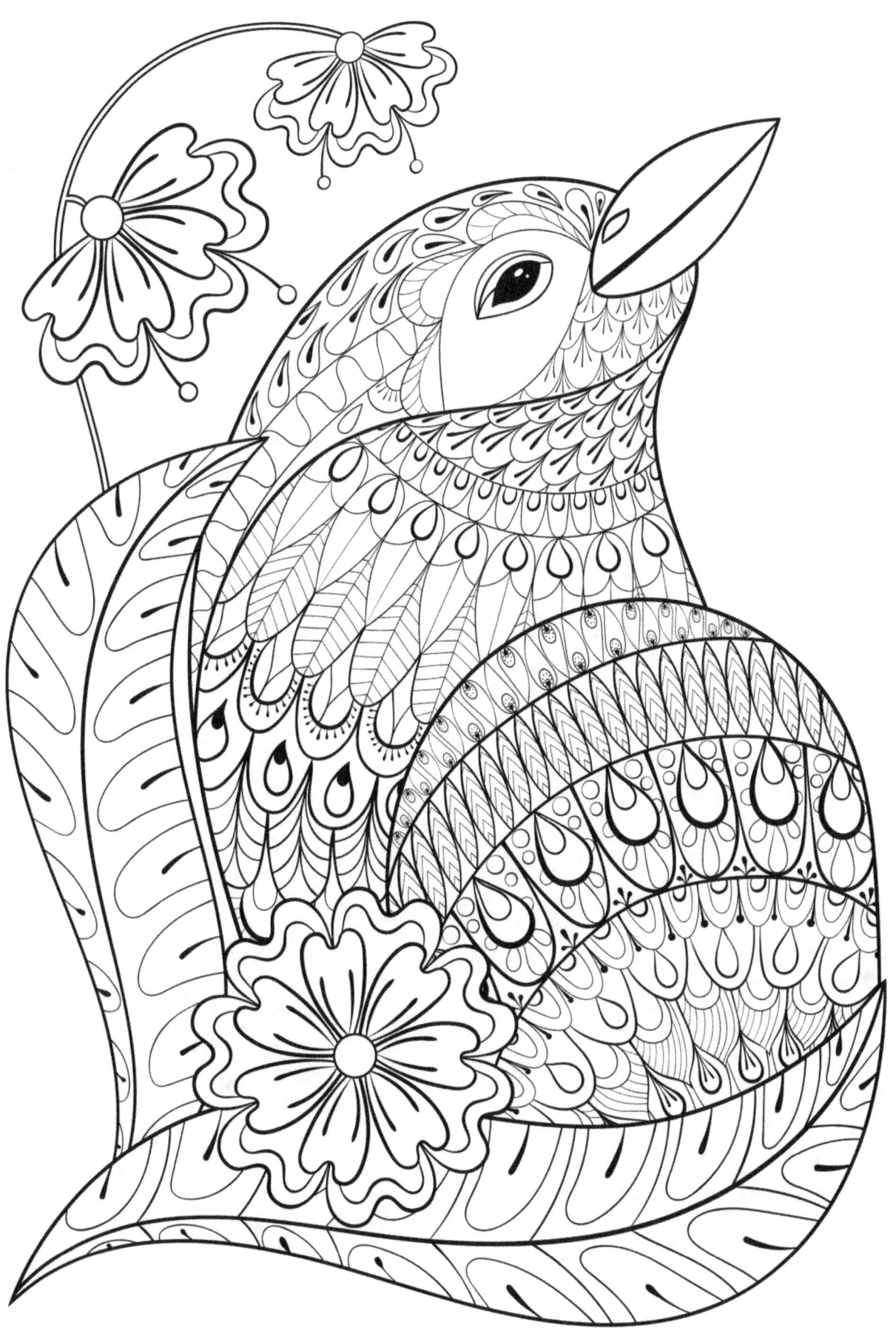

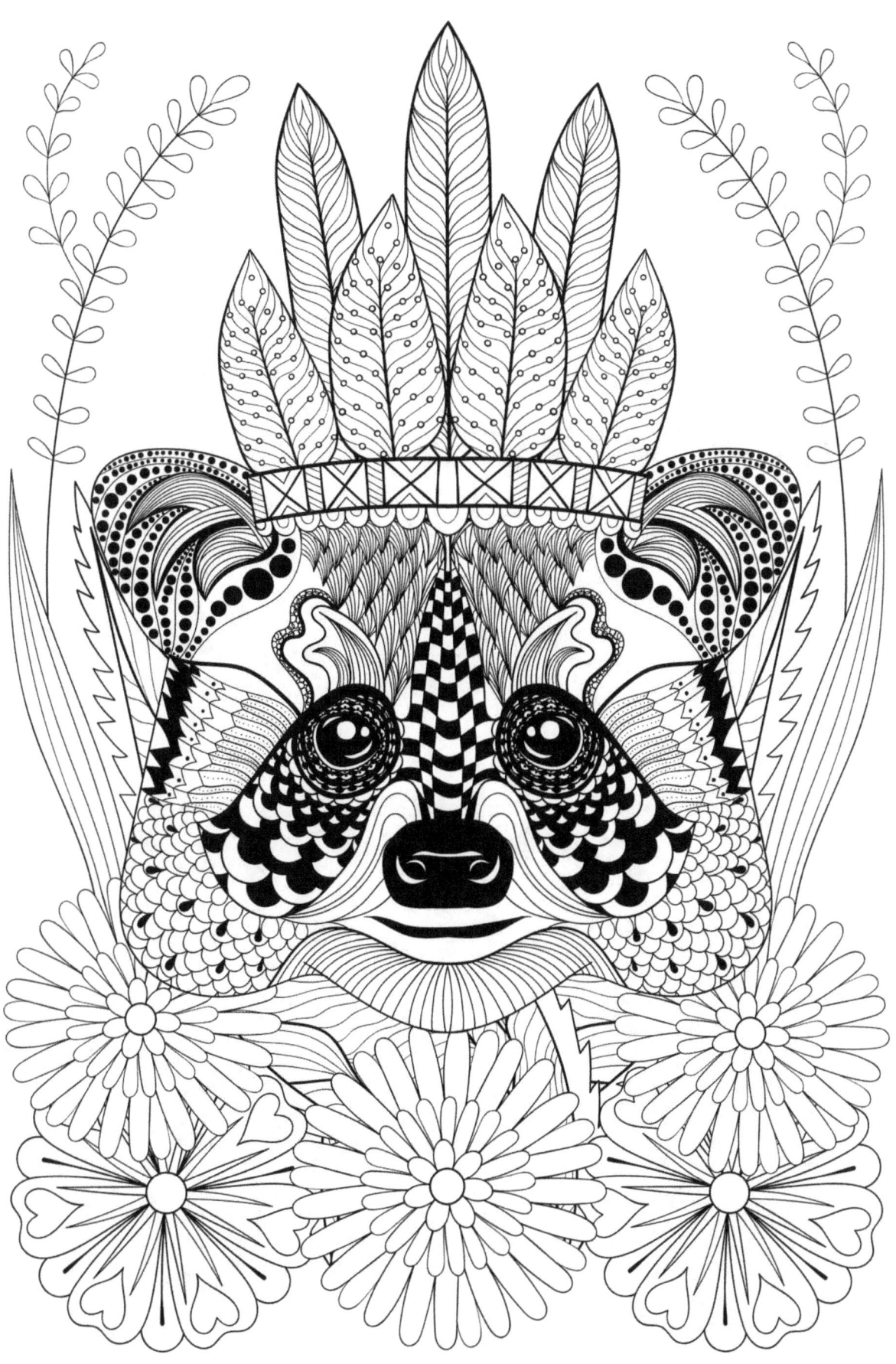

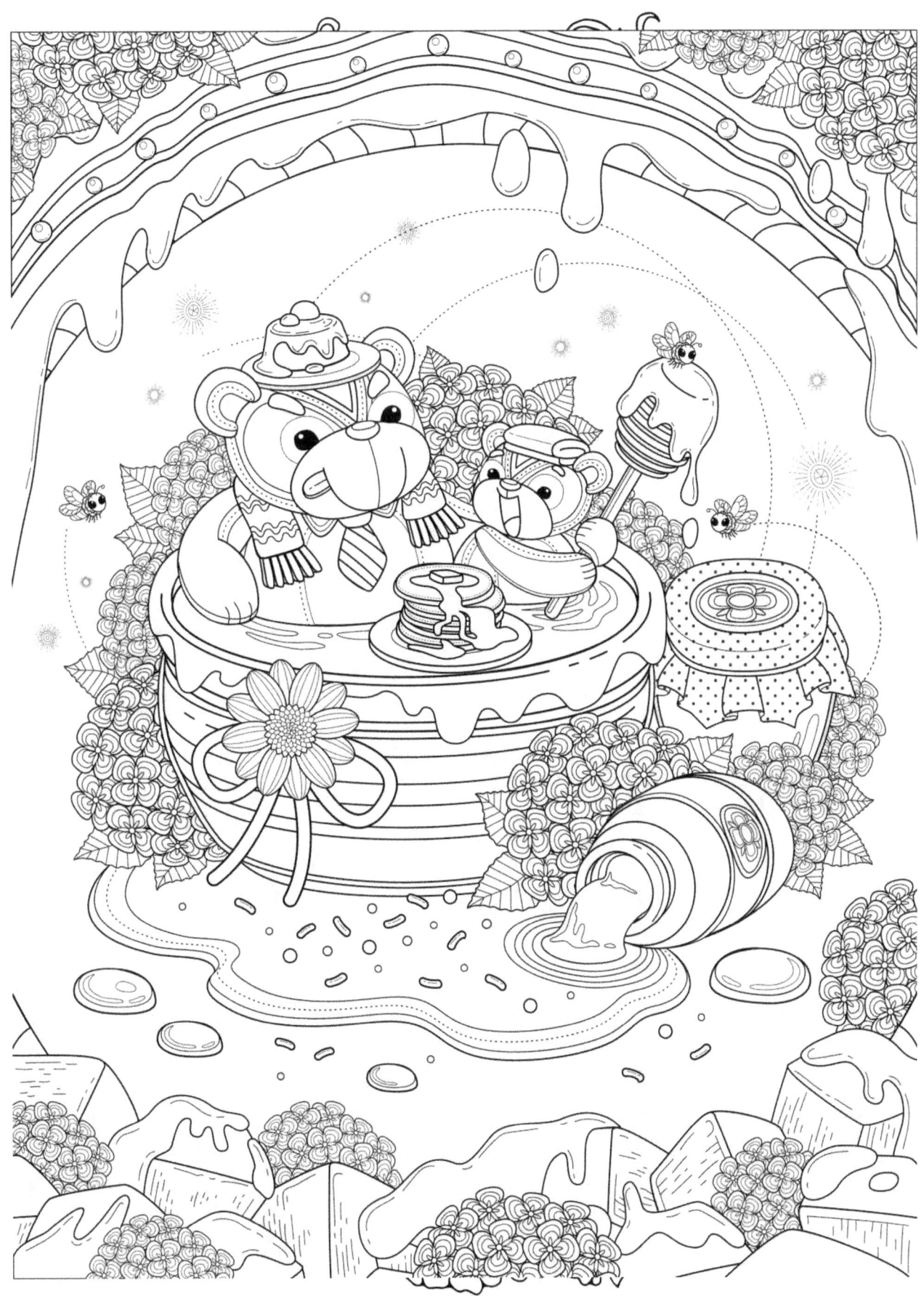

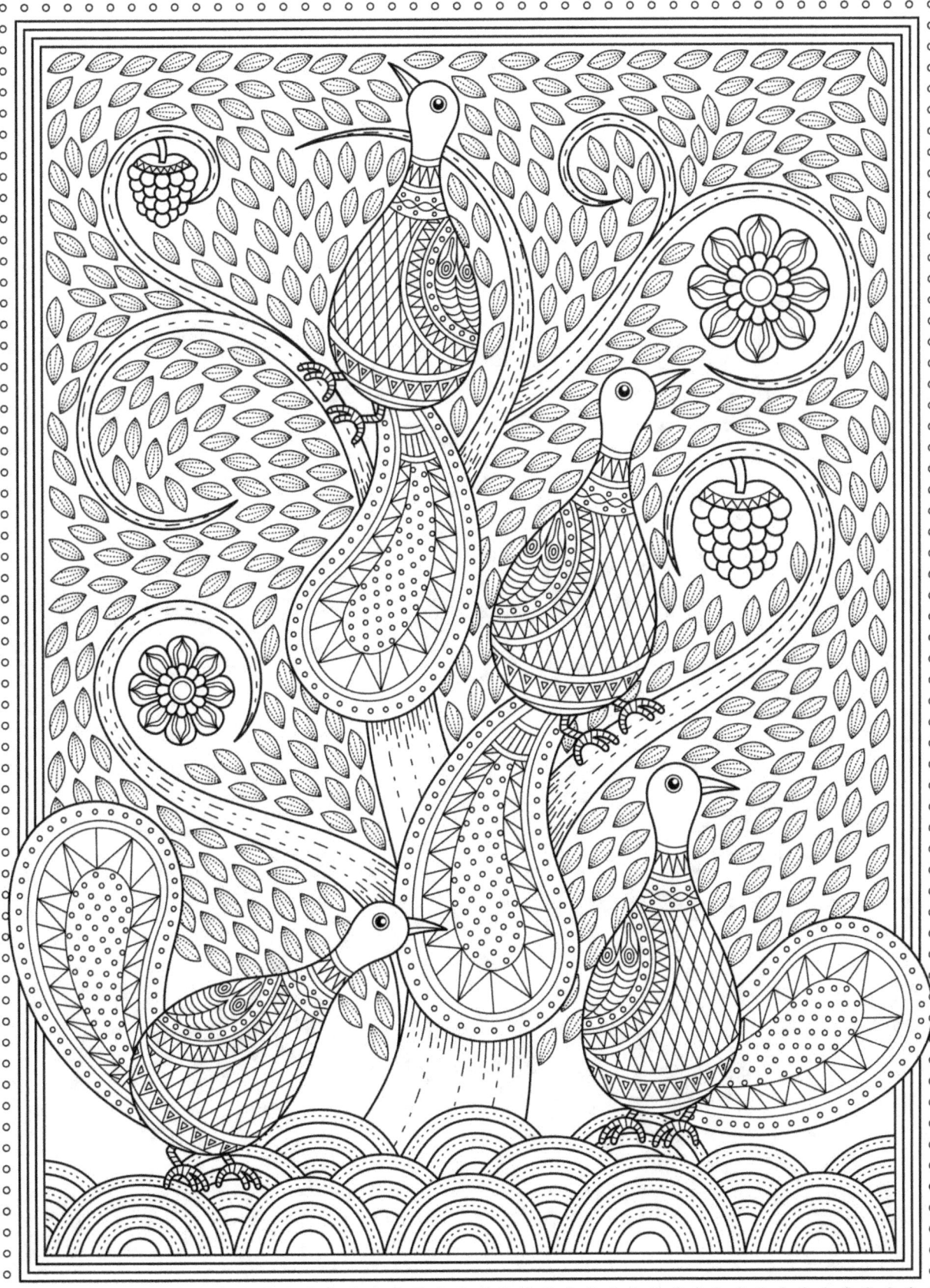

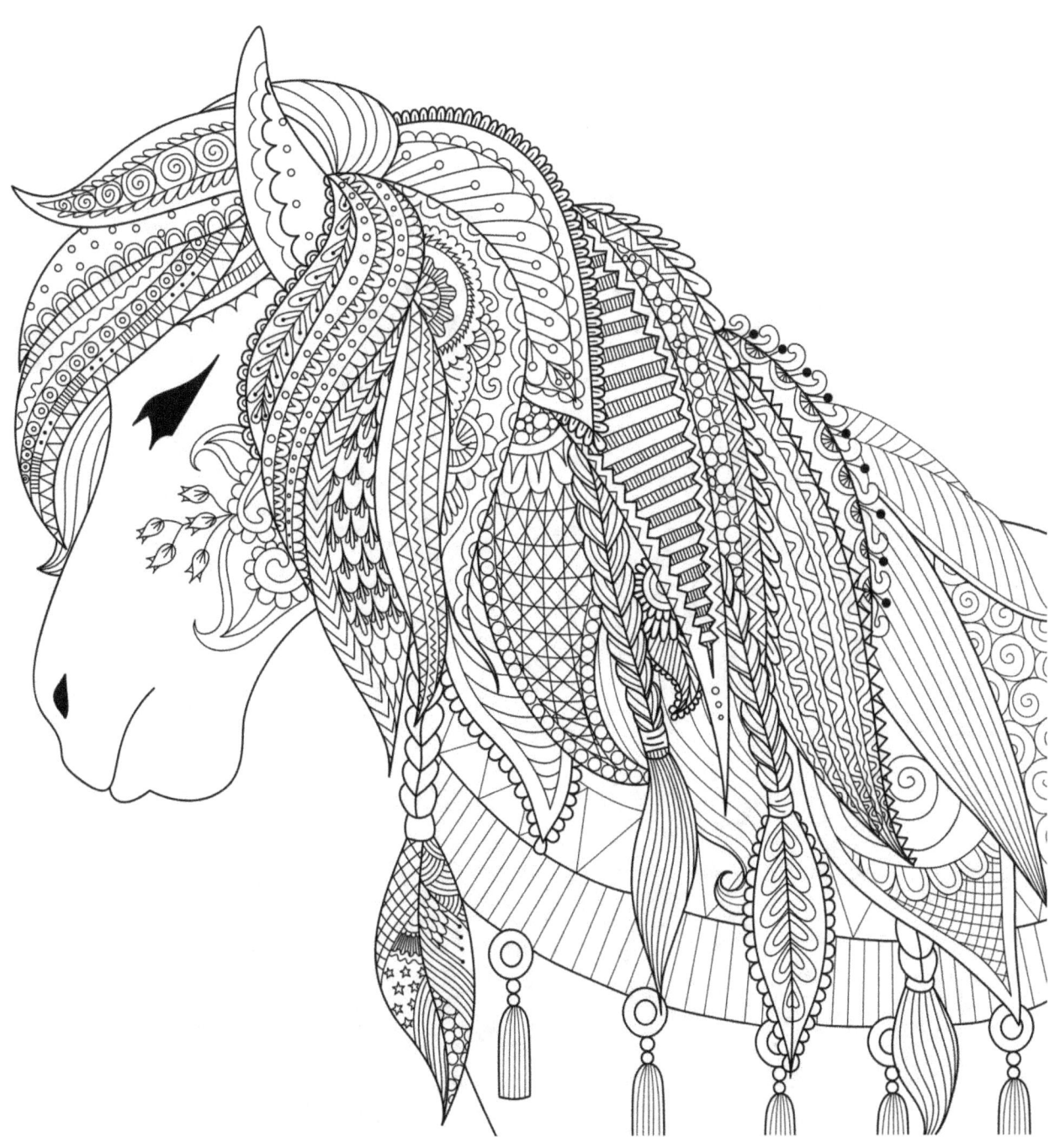

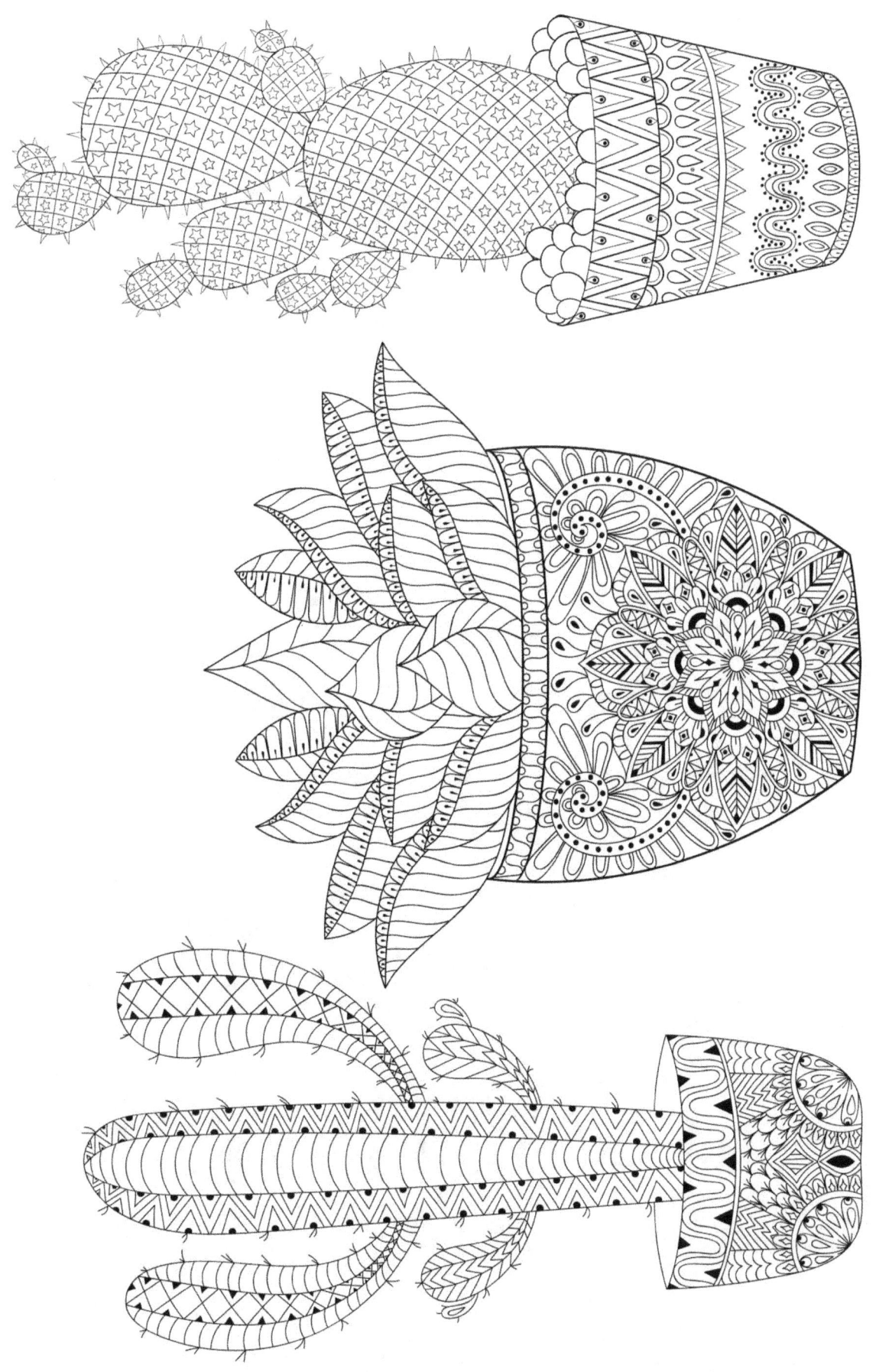

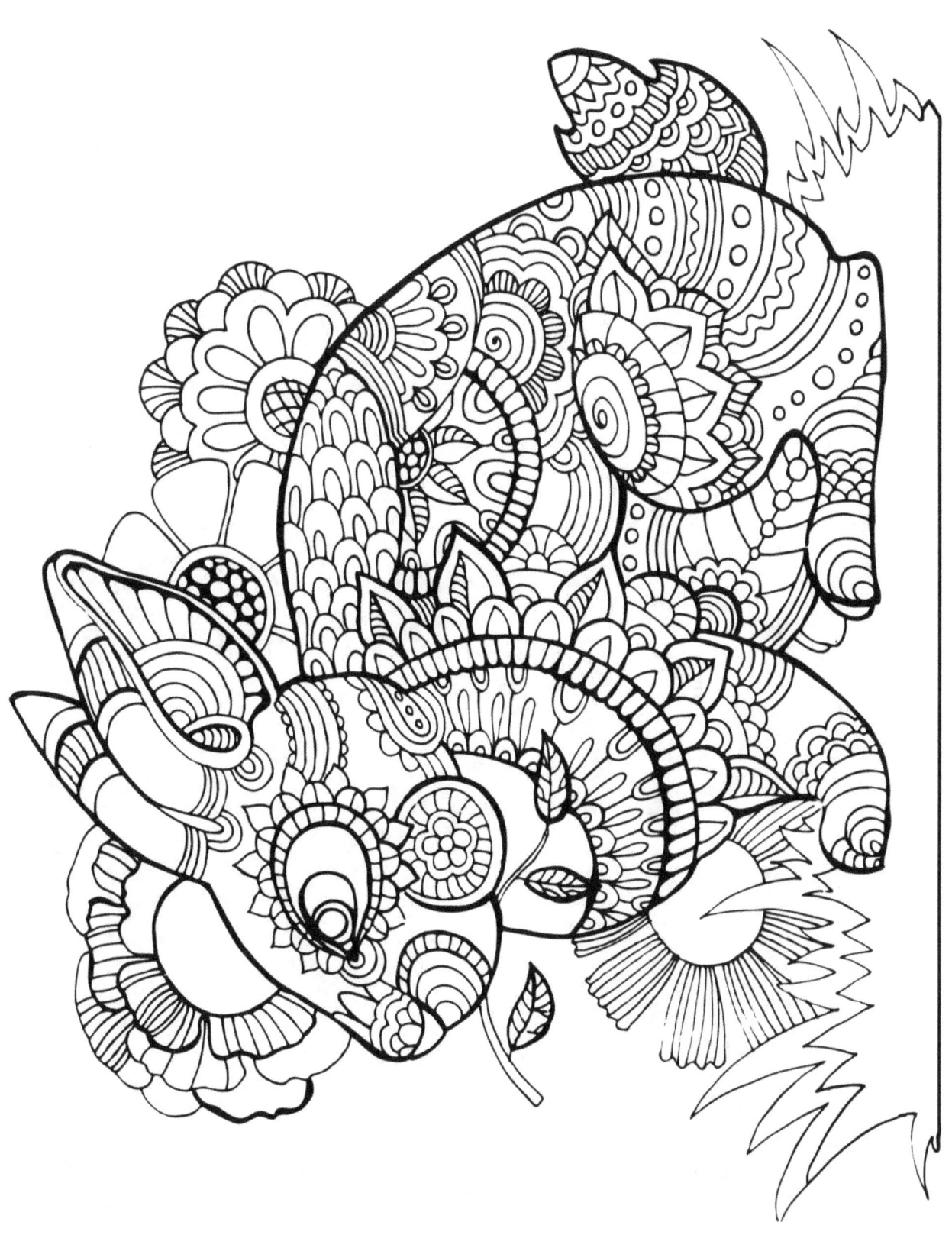

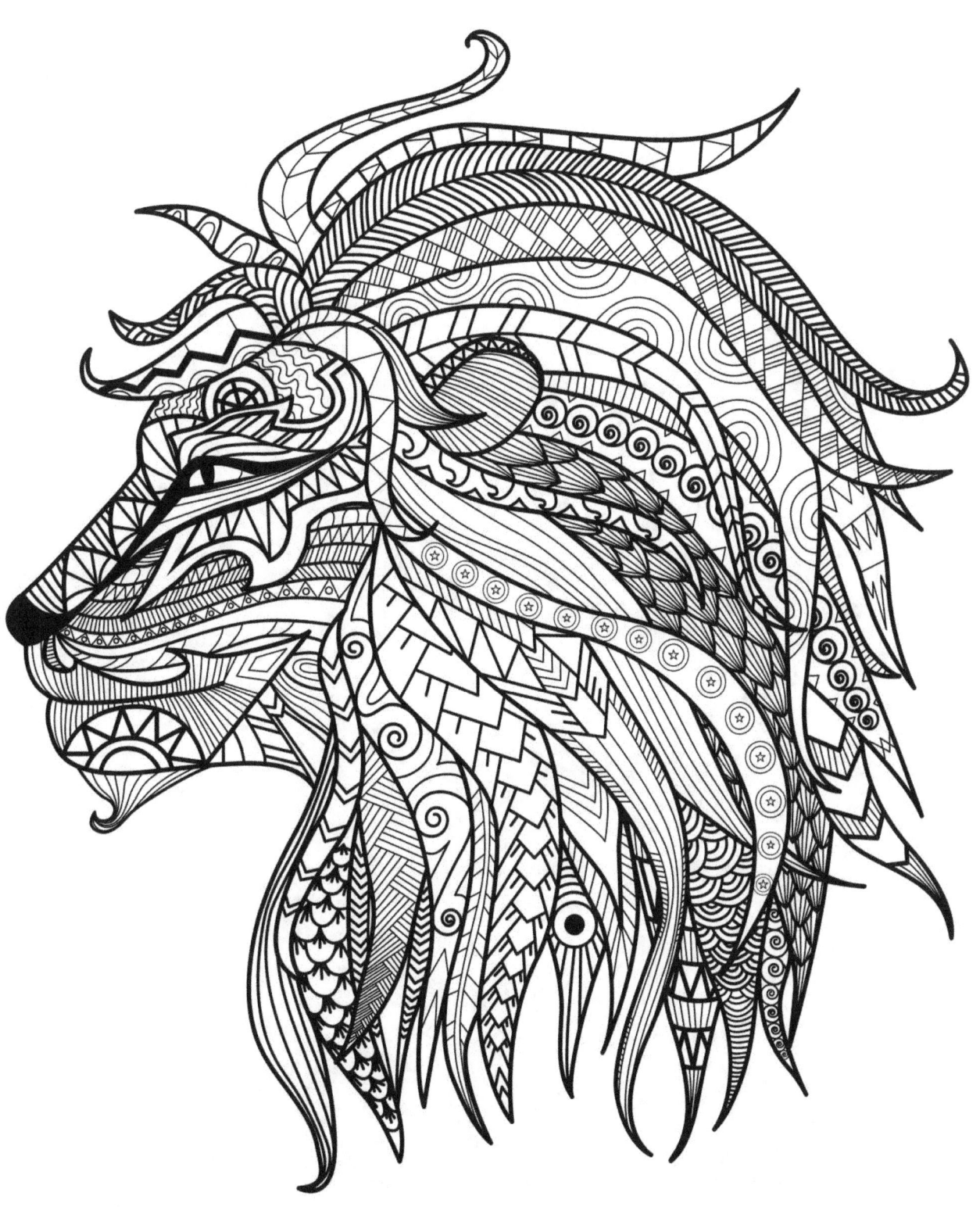

www.ingramcontent.com/pod-product-compliance
Lightning Source LLC
Chambersburg PA
CBHW081852170526
45167CB00007B/2986